William Shakespeare

The Tempest

Edited

with a Theatre Commentary by

John Russell Brown

The Applause Shakespeare Library
The Tempest
Editor and General Series Editor: John Russell Brown
Copyright © 1996 Applause Books

Library of Congress Cataloging-in-Publication Data

Shakespeare, William. 1564-1616.
    The Tempest / William Shakespeare ; Edited with a theatre commentary
by John Russell Brown.
        p.   cm. -- (The Applause Shakespeare library)
    Includes bibliographical references (p.).
    ISBN 1-55783-182-3 : $7.95
    I. Brown, John Russell. II. Title. III. Series.
PR2833.A2B76   1994
822.3'3--dc20   94-30103
                                            CIP

British Library Cataloging-in-Publication Data

A catalog record for this book is available from the British Library.

Applause Books	Combined Book Services Ltd
151 West 46th Street	Units I/K Paddock Wood Dist. Cen
New York, NY 10036	Tonbridge Kent TN12 6UU
Phone (212) 575-9265	Phone 01892 837171
Fax: (646) 562-5852	Fax 01892 837272

Cover photo from the Stratford Festival Production of *The Tempest*, Stratford, Ontario, 1976, Directed by Robin Phillips and William Hutt; Photograph by Robert C. Ragsdale.
From left: William Hutt (Prospero), Marti Maraden (Miranda)

Table of Contents

The Applause Shakespeare Library

Titles now Available:

King Lear
Macbeth
A Midsummer Night's Dream
The Tempest

Other Titles in Preparation

Antony and Cleopatra
Hamlet
Henry V
Julius Caesar
Measure for Measure
The Merchant of Venice
Othello
Romeo and Juliet
Twelfth Night

General Preface to the Applause Shakespeare Library

This edition is designed to help readers see and hear the plays in action. It gives an impression of how actors can bring life to the text and shows how certain speeches, movements, or silences take on huge importance once the words have left the page and become part of a performance. It is a theatrical edition, like no other available at this time.

Everyone knows that Shakespeare wrote for performance and not for solitary readers or students in classrooms. Yet the great problem of how to publish the plays so that readers can understand their theatrical life is only beginning to be tackled. Various solutions have been tried. The easiest—and it is an uneasy compromise—is to commission some director or leading actor to write a preface about the play in performance and print that at the beginning of the volume, followed by a critical and historical introduction, the text and notes about verbal difficulties, a textual introduction, and a collation of variant readings as in any other edition. Another easy answer is to supply extensive stage directions to sort out how characters enter or exit and describe any gestures or actions that the text explicitly requires. Both methods give the reader little or no help in realizing the play in performance, moment by moment, as the text is read.

A more thorough-going method is to include some notes about staging and acting among the annotations of meaning, topical references, classical allusions, textual problems, and so forth. The snag here is that the theatrical details make no consecutive sense and cannot deal with the larger issues of the build-up of conflict or atmosphere, the developing impression of character, or the effect of group and individual movement on stage. Such notes offer, at best, intermittent assistance.

In the more expensive one-volume editions, with larger-than-usual formats, yet another method is used—to include a stage history of the play showing how other ages have staged the play and describing a few recent productions that have been more than usually successful with the critics. The snag here is that unavailable historical knowledge is required to interpret records of earlier performances. Moreover, the journalistic accounts of productions which are quoted in these histories are liable to emphasize what is unusual in a production rather than the opportunities offered to actors in any production of the play, the text's enduring theatrical vitality. In any case, all this material is kept separate from the rest of the book and not easily consulted during a reading of the text.

The Applause Shakespeare goes further than any of these. It does the usual tasks expected of a responsible, modern edition, but adds a very special feature: a continuous commentary on the text by a professional director or a leading actor that considers the stage life of the play as its action unfolds. It shows what is demanded from the actors—line by line where necessary—and points out what decisions about interpretation have to be made and the consequences of one choice over another. It indicates where emotional climaxes are placed—and where conflicting thoughts in the character's mind create subtextual pressures beneath the words. Visual statements are noted: the effect of groups of figures on stage, of an isolated figure, or of a pair of linked figures in a changing relationship; the effect of delayed or unexpected entries, sudden departures, slow or processional exeunts, or a momentarily empty stage. Everything that happens on stage comes within the notice of this commentary. A reader can "feel" what the play would be like in action.

What the commentary does not do is equally important from the reader's point of view. It does not try to provide a single theatrical reading of the text. Rather if offers a range of possibilities, a number of suggestions as to what an actor might do. Performances cannot be confined to a single, unalterable realization: rather, each production is continually discovering new potential in a text, and it is this power of revelation and revaluation that the commentary of the Applause Shakespeare seeks to open up to individual readers. With this text in hand, the play can be produced in the theatre of the mind, creating a performance suitable to the moment and responsive to individual imaginations. As stimulus for such recreations, the commentary sometimes describes the choices that particular actors or directors made in famous productions, showing what effect words or physical performances have achieved. The purpose here is to supplement what a reader might supply from his or her own experience and imagination, and also to suggest ways in which further research might discover more about the text's theatrical life.

The commentary is printed in a wide column on the page facing the text itself, so that reference can be quickly made at any particular point or, alternatively, so that the commentary can be read as its own narrative of the pay in action. Also, to the right of the text are explanations of difficult words, puns, multiple meanings, topical allusions, references to other texts, etc. All of these things will be found in other editions, but here it is readily accessible without the eye having to seek out the foot of the page or notes bunched together at the rear of the volume. The text is modernized in spelling. Both stage directions and punctuation are kept to a minimum—enough to make reading easy, but not so elaborate that readers are prevented from giving life to the text in whatever way they choose. As an aid to reading aloud, speech-prefixes are printed in full and extra space used to set speeches apart from each other; when the text is read silently, each new voice can register clearly. At the rear of the book, an extended note explains the authority for the text and a collation gives details of variant readings and emendations.

In many ways the Applause Shakespeare is a pioneering edition, responding to an old challenge in a new way and trying to break down barriers to understanding that have proved very obstinate for a long time. Further volumes are in preparation and editorial procedures are being kept under review. Reports on the usefulness of the edition, and especially of its theatrical commentary, would be most welcome. Please write to John Russell Brown, c/o Applause Books, 151 West 46th Street, 8th Floor, New York, NY 10036.

INTRODUCTION

None of Shakespeare's plays is "so baffling and elusive as *The Tempest*," wrote Peter Brook, the director of four remarkable productions of this comedy. But its power is as noticeable as its mystery, and Brook also believes that this is Shakespeare's "complete and final statement, and that it deals with the whole condition of man."[1] Unlock this puzzle and a world of understanding may lie before you.

For Shakespeare himself, it must have been a very special play. He worked on it during the years 1610 and 1611, at a time when he was retiring from life in London and taking up permanent residence with his wife in his home at Stratford-upon-Avon. He may have thought of *The Tempest* as the last play he would ever write; certainly nothing has survived from the next year, while from the succeeding years until his death in 1623 we know only the history play *Henry VIII*, which he wrote in collaboration with a much younger writer, John Fletcher, and two minor collaborations, *The Two Noble Kinsmen* and the no longer extant *Cardenio,* both with Fletcher. The character at the center of the play, Prospero, dominates all the action and most actors, readers, and playgoers will suspect that Shakespeare identified strongly with this thoughtful and deeply involved man who combines the roles of father, ruler, and magician. Prospero, in charge of the island on which he has been shipwrecked, is like a dramatist in charge of a play: noise, music, change of scene, action, marvels, and human encounters all occur as he wills them. He arranges a last scene in which all the other characters come together, and then he asks for applause from the audience. The eloquent soliloquy in which he says farewell to the spirits who have served him (V.i.33–57) can be understood as Shakespeare's farewell to his art.

But *The Tempest* is not a perfunctory or self-indulgent valediction, nor a graceful bowing-out. Prospero is onstage for three-fifths of the play and is continuously present from Act III, scene iii to the very end. He makes wonderful visions appear by magic, but he also calls into being frightening spectacles and provokes criminal activity, absurd acts of folly, and desperate madness. The play starts with a storm at sea in which men despair of

---

[1] *The Empty Space* (London, 1968), pp. 94–95.

their lives, and yet the greatest violence is within men's minds, especially within Prospero's; the man who raises the tempest is himself torn and turned around by forces which he has not anticipated. In one sense, the play shows the reformation, or regeneration, of Prospero, for only at the crisis at the beginning of Act V (ll. 17–20) does he listen to counsel and discover a need for tenderness and forgiveness. Until this moment, Prospero has believed he had the "power" (III.iii.90) to force his enemies into submission and reformation. Intent on a long-delayed "vengeance" (V.i.28) he controlled everyone, and everything, so that they would serve and obey him.

The dramatic techniques of this late play are as challenging as its themes and action. Shakespeare was breaking new ground, not repeating popular successes. For most of his plays, he borrowed a plot from earlier narrative or drama, but here the plot seems to have been entirely his own invention. It uses traditional elements, but in new guises and to new effects. What was conventionally serious is often made to look ridiculous, what was funny is here enacted in desperate circumstances. The action is highly concentrated, all taking place on or around one island and in four consecutive hours; in this Shakespeare conformed to classical notions of unity instead of exploiting the freedom of popular and narrative dramatic example, as in all his other mature plays. The whole design and the incidental invention are both unexpected, and are both brilliantly executed. One character is invisible at will, another is both beast and man. Music and dance are used in a variety of ways, comical and satirical, as well as ceremonial and supernatural. New modes of soliloquy and silence, long expository speeches, denigratory asides and simultaneous speeches, inarticulate cries and instantaneous shifts of mood, and words used in new senses or new forms are among the many indications of the dramatist's insistent creative energy.

The challenge of performing this text has been so great that for some centuries after Shakespeare's own time it was never entirely accepted. The play was altered for production, by omissions and by long additions which exploited a new taste for opera and topical political satire. The dramatists William Davenant (1606–68), John Dryden (1631–1700), and Thomas Shadwell (1642?–92) gave it new characters and a new title, *The Enchanted Island*. Henry Purcell (1659–95) wrote extensive music. Occasionally during the eighteenth century a return was made to Shakespeare's text—it was cheaper to stage than the more elaborate adaptations—but not until a production by William Macready in 1838 at the Covent Garden Theatre was the play habitually seen in the original version. But now it was a scenic triumph, with a device for flying and a setting full of picturesque rocks and sea-shore; the shipwreck of the first scene was staged so realistically, according to the fashion of the times, that the words were lost.

In the twentieth century, *The Tempest* has been more frequently performed than ever before, and usually with most of Shakespeare's text intact. Small-scale experimental theatres have been drawn to it and also the grandest "festival" theatres which can stage it with every mechanical and electronic accessory. Yet almost always it eludes a fully acceptable realization; unlike the other best-known plays, it has not been seen in a production which was universally hailed as a masterpiece. "How often one sees *The Tempest*," wrote one disenchanted drama critic, "and how rarely is one satisfied with it in performance:" for "the essential magic" we are often given merely stage "tricks."[2]

Above all, Shakespeare has made unprecedented demands on actors, calling for exceptional talents and unselfish performances. When Arnold Moss played Prospero on Broadway in Margaret Webster's 1945 production, he found that all the scholars and critics he had read were too limited to be of much use: "like the seven blind men of India, Prospero was for each of them a different part of the elephant, while none had seen him whole" (*Theatre Arts*). This actor was among those who have played Prospero as a vigorous, energetic prince in his forties. So was Morris Carnovsky at Stratford, Connecticut, in 1960, but he offset obvious pride with a "great magnanimity" and added an impatience, "as a rather exacting teacher may be impatient with slow learners" (*Christian Science Monitor*). At Stratford-upon-Avon in 1982, Derek Jacobi was both vigorous and tormented; he was glad "to shed the burden of his magic" and was "not afraid to shout, weep, or show weakness" (*Shakespeare Survey*).

Other actors have emphasized Prospero's occult powers, attempting to portray a wholly exceptional and mystical genius. Charles Laughton, in 1934, had the appearance of the Ancient of Days in the visionary drawings of the poet William Blake (1757–1827). A variation of this was the austere, aesthetic, and misanthropic recluse: John Gielgud, in 1957, seemed to live "under the threat of being engulfed by his sense of being wronged....He has to fight against the temptation to give way to it"; his magic led him into "fearful territory; he is perhaps as frightened of his powers as he is proud of

---

[2] *Financial Times* (London), 3 April 1963.

them" (*New Statesman*). When this Prospero renounced his magic powers, relief seemed stronger than regret. Playing the role again, for the National Theatre in London in 1974, Gielgud's magician was seen as "an explorer of the possibilities and limits of art" who at the close of the play "begs the audience 'to set me *free*'" (*Plays and Players*). Michael Redgrave's Prospero was absorbed in his visions: "while his hands were at their craft, his head was in the air, as if peering after the ultimate" (*Birmingham Post*); "each feat of magic was in doubt until it had triumphed and...the achievement was paid for by an ensuing exhaustion" (*Times*, London).

In contrast to all these, Michael Bryant's Prospero at the National Theatre in 1988 was "embittered and embattled, but seeking new life" (*Financial Times*); he was "no longer a seraphic mage and un-political bookworm, but an impious magician devoured with hatred for the usurpers who have at last fallen into his power." He was a "tortured human being": he whispered "Graves at my command Have wak'd their sleepers", as though "expecting a thunderbolt to fall on him"; it was not a farewell to art but "a confession of blasphemy" (*Times*, London).

The exceptional demands on the actor of Prospero are evident in the very plot of the play. He commands supernatural spirits like a renaissance Magus, a man to whom self-discipline, learning, and wisdom have given a "natural" power over the demons that were thought to inhabit the physical world; such a man could foretell the future and understand all the functions of the universe, and was close to the very being of God. This magician, aided by Ariel, an especially "delicate" or refined spirit, brings his enemies and one old friend to the island on which he had landed twelve years previously, accompanied by his only child Miranda. He hates the brother who had deposed him from his throne as fervently as he loves his daughter. His hopes for the future depend on arranging for this child to marry the son of one of his enemies. Moreover, Prospero has made himself ruler of the island and is responsible for its good order: he has dispossessed Caliban, the witch's son who lived there when he first arrived, but has failed to teach him obedience or restrain him from violence; he therefore forces him into submission. After suffering intense anger and terrorizing all those who resist him, Prospero has to achieve some measure of reconciliation with his world and with himself; and this involves the renunciation of magical powers and a return to his native Milan.

After Prospero, the next biggest demands are made on the actors of Ariel and Caliban. The text of the play does not make absolutely clear how either of these should look or what should be their physical characteristics. Ariel was originally played by a boy actor and has been given to both actors and actresses. In 1934, Elsa Lanchester, in metallic paint, was a "rare creature with extreme swiftness, lightness, vitality, grace" (*Times*, London): she "maintained throughout a birdlike reserve; malice and loyalty alike were tinged with a kind of remoteness" (*Spectator*). A complete contrast to this interpretation was Ben Kingsley's Ariel, at the Royal Shakespeare Theatre, Stratford-upon-Avon in 1970. He was a "slow moving, secretive native servant, naked except for a G string and a Sioux hairpiece, suggesting the victims depicted in those ancient prints of the Conquest of the Americas. He used a weird falsetto voice" (*Guardian*). Nicholas Pennell at Stratford, Ontario, in 1976 combined something of both these; he was a "white creature, a captive spirit who walked with the tentative steps of a tall bird, body rigid, moving the legs only. Stone-white, motionless and attentive much of the time, when he moved it was as if a portion of the air had taken form and motion" (*Shakespeare Quarterly*).

Since he is an "airy" spirit, Ariel should possibly be capable of taking many different "shapes," obedient to the fancies and desires of Prospero. So Michael Feast's "quicksilver" Ariel at the National Theatre in 1974, "whether descending as a white Cupid from the heavens, or garbed as a Botticelli-like androgyne, addressing Ferdinand in a perfect counter-tenor, or inciting the clowns to further idiocies as a haunted jester—this Ariel never resembles the faceless ethereal spirit of conventional productions" (*Plays and Players*). He also appeared as a Harpy and as the goddess Ceres. However he has been cast and dressed, Ariel has to move quickly from one mood to another, responding wholly to what he sees and hears, laughing, singing, groaning, mimicking, pleading, denouncing, seducing.

Caliban is half-mortal and that much easier to visualize and cast than the spirit Ariel. But productions have shown an even wider spectrum of shapes and styles. In the nineteenth century, Caliban was played by the famous comedian William Burton in his own theatre in New York. Burton excelled in extravagant farce, but he was also a master of simple, natural pathos; he was rotund and had a remarkably strong and clear voice. When he played Caliban, "a wild creature on all fours sprang upon the stage, with claws on his hands....It was a creature of the woods, one of nature's spawns;

it...rubbed itself against the backs of trees."[3] In the present century, Henry Bayton hired the Savoy Theatre in London especially to act his own version of Caliban: "a wild, uncanny animal, reminding one of a wrathful brute kicking and revolting against the bars of the Zoo.... He moaned and groaned and panted and raged" (*Sketch*). Bayton emphasized the "monstrosity" of the role and halfway through the play he brought down the curtain "sensationally...by seizing a snake and chewing the wriggling reptile between his teeth" (*Sunday Pictorial*). This Caliban was seen on the island after the end of the play and the performance ended as he swallowed a live fish. Sir Herbert Beerbohm Tree had previously taken the liberty of ending the play with Caliban played by himself, but when he returned to the empty stage it was to look "yearningly after the ship that carried the rest of the cast away from the island."[4]

But few Calibans have been the main attraction of the play. Usually he is played in strong contrast with Ariel, so that one reflects Prospero's imaginative thoughts and the other the "baser" instincts of humanity. Roy Dotrice, at Stratford-upon-Avon in 1963, was "lean, dark-skinned, practically naked with running sores;" he appeared at first "gnawing an enormous bone, later to be used for an effective phallic gesture"; yet he was, for most of the play, "terrified" (*The Stage*). At the same theatre, seven years later, Barry Stanton's Caliban was grotesque and helpless, "flopping squatly about like a huge sea-elephant pathetically trying to imitate his fellow servant's songs" (*Observer*). At Stratford Connecticut in 1955, Jack Palance made Caliban strange and fantastic, being "weirdly costumed in fish scales and huge clawed hands and feet" (*New York Herald Tribune*); he was a "whining, pathetically subnormal creature," with a touch of the "Hollywood ogre" about him (*Variety*). Richard Burton's Caliban at the Old Vic Theatre, London, in 1954, was much more likable; an "adorable monster, like a lumbering pet dog" (*Plays and Players*)—but at the end of the play he strode off "carrying two men aloft like dumb-bells" (*Daily Express*).

The effect of Caliban, and the balance of the whole play, depends on whether more emphasis is given to his brutishness and violence or to his helplessness and simplicity. Despite a costume which made him look like a "cross between a turtle and a lizard," Earl Hyman at Stratford, Connecticut, in 1960 was "deeply touching in his pathetic attempts to assert himself"

---

[3] *Actors and Actresses*, ed. B. Matthews and L. Hutton (New York), iii. 231.
[4] H. Pearson, *Beerbohm Tree* (London, 1956), p. 132.

(*Variety*). In some productions, Caliban has had the appearance and behavior of the "savages" described by Jacobean colonizers of North America and Prospero's enslavement of him seems totally unreasonable and tyrannical. (We know that Shakespeare borrowed details from a colonist's account of a voyage to the Bermudas for the storm of scene i and that he quoted Montaigne's essay "Of Cannibals," as translated by John Florio and published in 1603, for Gonzalo's talk of the "plantation" of the island in II.i.) At the National Theatre in London in 1988, Tony Haygarth's Caliban was "blood-caked" from the tortures of his slavery and very much the "undeserving victim" of his master (*Times*, London).

Other characters in the play are less difficult to pin down. The difficulty they present is a shortage of words: each has deeply-felt and strong feelings but these are not expressed through abundant imagery and sustained speech. Alonso, the King of Naples, should dominate the stage-picture when he arrives with his courtiers on the "bare island" in II.i; he is their master, and his own feelings of grief and guilt are essential for the scene's development. But this character has only some twenty lines, out of the three hundred and eleven that make up the scene, and only two of his speeches are longer than two verse-lines: timing, rhythm, inward reactions, suppressed emotion, physical bearing and actions, together with the careful pointing of words and phrases, are all of crucial importance in creating the role and the appropriate dynamics for the scene.

Other characters talk about matters of secondary importance and at moments of crisis may become frenzied, silent, or extremely terse. Yet there is little doubt that they have been imagined ambitiously and clearly, because they repay thorough exploration in rehearsal and sharp performances. Arthur Lowe, as the drunken butler, Stephano, at the National Theatre in 1974, seemed about to "turn into a mini-Macbeth at the prospect of becoming the ruler of the island" (*Plays and Players*). Cyril Cusack's Antonio in the same production, bore "all the cynical distinguishing marks" of the large-scale political portraits in Shakespeare's history plays (*ibid.*). Alonso's brother, Sebastian, interacts with Antonio in a most subtle way, seeming to be the more slothful of the two, but probing with accuracy into political appearances and assuming initiative when he is ready with compact and compelling echoes of Macbeth (see commentary on II.i.224–87; III.iii.1–10; V.i.277–81).

Miranda and Ferdinand, the two young lovers, meet each other under the gaze and control of Prospero and fall headlong into amazement and transforming love: the girl sees the first man in her whole life (other than Caliban and her father), while the young prince believes his father and all his companions have been drowned and doubts whether Miranda can be a human being. Both parts need exceptional tact and truthfulness in performance.

Although they speak with lifelike immediacy and directness, the characters of this play are all involved in strange actions and unusual states of mind. They need to be carefully and boldly realized in performance. The whole drama seems, in its mixture of fantasy, sharp feeling, and rapid changes of mood and intention, to be a kind of dream. Shakespeare has brought politicians, autocrats, clowns, spirits, nonentities, and attendants to the stage and led them "through forthrights and meanders" (III.iii.3) towards an unmasking that they do not control and scarcely understand. Gonzalo tries to sum up the whole experience by saying that they have all "found" themselves, "when no man was his own" (V.i.208–13). But such a hopeful interpretation of events goes almost no distance towards helping an actor discover a suitable performance or a reader to become more aware of the pressures that lie behind the words of Shakespeare's text.

In a program note for his production at the Guthrie Theatre, Minneapolis in 1982, Liviu Ciulei wrote that:

> Prospero's magic is for me a metaphor for the power of art: and his terrain is a studio or laboratory where he, the magician-artist-scientist, will explore the limits of Man's mind, soul and morality....Can art assist in today's struggle between rationality and instinct, community and alienation, civilization and barbarism? Can art help to return to Man his own majesty?

For all the compact unity of the play's action, its text comes fully alive only when everyone involved in a production is willing to question the implications of each word and each sequence of fantastic events.

Particularly important for an appreciation of *The Tempest* are the visual aspects of its action. Characters have to be seen in their confrontations and changing states of awareness and being. That is true for any Shakespeare play, but here spectacle is a significant element in the very construction of the drama. Large stage-pictures sometimes take over from speech and individual action: Act IV, scene i, for example, requires stage devices, processional entries, dance, and music that were common in court masques during the reign of James I but comparatively rare in the plays of the Jacobean public theatres. In effect this scene contains a short masque introduced as an entertainment devised by Prospero for the newly betrothed Ferdinand and Miranda. Three goddesses, in elaborate costumes, make their stately entries, Juno in a chariot drawn by peacocks and descending from the "heavens" over the stage. Then two dancing and speechless choruses, one of nymphs and the other of sicklemen, fill the stage with contrasting movements and encounter each other in a dance. At least eleven, and probably nineteen, actors are required for this one incident, and these are in addition to the requirements of the *dramatis personae* of the play itself. Although on stage for only a short time, these dancer-actors are essential for establishing a more symbolic or ideal drama than is found elsewhere in Shakespeare's plays. It is both stately and directly related by its verbal imagery to the ordinary, everyday countryside of Shakespeare's England. Some of the words of its speeches and invocations are innovatory and consciously artificial (see the glossarial notes). The play stands still, as it were, for this inset vision, which is recognized by Ferdinand as "most majestic" and "harmonious charmingly" (IV.i.118–19).

The other spectacular scenes require more constant interplay with the *dramatis personae*. In Act I, scene i, Shakespeare has used the actor-dancers to crowd the stage with mariners, who haul on ropes, climb aloft, become drenched with water, and fall to their prayers. In Act III they become strange "shapes" who enter with a banquet, offering it with dance and silent gestures; then, as Ariel appears as a harpy, they remove the table with derisive gestures and grimaces. Finally, after the betrothal masque, the dancers become ravenous "hounds," called by such names as Mountain, Tyrant, Fury, and Silver (the poisonous quicksilver); like the hounds of heaven they pursue Caliban and his confederates, Stephano and the fool Trinculo, who are set roaring like the storm itself (compare I.i.15 and IV.i.259).

The action of *The Tempest* is, then, diversified and given shape by four, full-scale spectacular scenes which involve concerted actions, music, and noise. It is noticeable that the stage directions and text for these incidents echo each other precisely in describing the appearances and sounds. The most elaborate of them, the masque, is not completed, but just before the dancers have reached the stately culmination of their "encounters" (IV.i.137), Prospero intervenes so that the "graceful" image of reconciliation of contrasting elements—water and air, represented by the nymphs, and earth and fire, by the sicklemen—is destroyed by Prospero's memory of the beast Caliban and by his own anger. As the dancers "heavily vanish," there is a "strange, hollow, and confused noise" that echoes both the initial storm at sea and the temptation presented by the "strange shapes" and dominated by the harpy. The next spectacular incident represents the violence of hunting, with "Prospero and Ariel *setting them on*."

When Shakespeare's play was adapted into an opera or musical, by Dryden, Shadwell, and Purcell, the most notable "improvement" was the addition of a further spectacular scene, "The Masque of Neptune," to carry on the sequence and conclude the entertainment fittingly. This change draws attention to what must have seemed very odd to *The Tempest*'s first audiences and was perhaps one of Shakespeare's most original artistic decisions. A full conclusion, something still more elaborate, seems needed—in the manner of Hymen's entry at the end of *As You Like It* or the pageant and songs of *Love's Labor's Lost*. At the beginning of the last Act, words and actions seem to indicate that such a *finale* is on its way: Prospero calls for solemn music (see V.i.52) and draws a circle on the stage. He changes his clothes in order to appear as a "prince of power," and this has a musical accompaniment. He also takes in his hand a sword, symbol of retribution. Then all Prospero's enemies enter and are held still and silent in the circle, controlled by magic. To all appearances this is a preparation for a final irresistible confrontation, a masque in which justice is vindicated. But it is not. None of these characters is compelled to do anything. No spirits enter to encounter them or establish an elaborate image of past, present, or future. Rather the music stops, and each of them reawakens to their lives as best he may. All that Prospero "discovers," by moving up-stage and drawing a curtain, is Ferdinand and Miranda sitting together and playing chess. The men who stand in a circle and the others who subsequently enter, drawn or driven by Ariel, have to be themselves. They become aware of survival, each other, and forgiveness. They move onwards with their limited resources and usual misunderstandings. Each reacts in his own imperfect way while the one remaining spirit flies off, free "to the elements."

Prospero's last words in the play are "Please you, draw near" as he invites the assembled company to his cell, so there is one more entirely silent visual effect, but it is not controlled by a magician. One by one, in their own time, they walk past Prospero and must greet—or refuse to greet—their host in whatever way they find appropriate. Then Prospero returns to face the theatre audience alone. The actor speaks in his own person as well as for Prospero:

> Now my charms are all o'erthrown,
> And what strength I have's mine own,
> Which is most faint....

This, the most splendid and artificial of Shakespeare's plays, and the most mysterious and dreamlike, ends with a man asking to be accepted as a man, in understanding and indulgence. Sometimes this quiet and intimate moment stays in our minds after all the gorgeous visions of the revels have melted away: it seems as if we have been asked to recognize and understand our neighbors and ourselves.

The Tempest

CHARACTERS

ALONSO, King of Naples
SEBASTIAN, his brother
PROSPERO, the right Duke of
  Milan
ANTONIO, his brother, the
  usurping Duke of Milan
FERDINAND, son to the King of
  Naples
GONZALO, an honest old
  councilor
ADRIAN } LORDS
FRANCISCO }
CALIBAN, a savage and
  deformed slave

TRINCULO, a jester
STEPHANO, a drunken butler
MASTER of a ship
BOATSWAIN
MARINERS

MIRANDA, daughter to Prospero

ARIEL, an airy spirit
IRIS
CERES
JUNO   } [characters in the
NYMPHS   masque, played
REAPERS   by] SPIRITS

[Other SPIRITS, in the service of Prospero]

SCENE   *An uninhabited island*

ACT I

Scene i   *A tempestuous noise of thunder and lightning heard. Enter a* SHIPMASTER° *and a* BOATSWAIN.°

MASTER   Boatswain!

BOATSWAIN   Here master. What cheer?°

MASTER   Good: speak to° th' mariners. Fall to't, yarely,° or we run ourselves aground. Bestir, bestir!   *Exit.*

Enter MARINERS.

BOATSWAIN   Heigh my hearts! Cheerly,° cheerly my hearts! Yare,   5
yare! Take in the topsail.° Tend to° th' master's whistle!—

"*SCENE* An uninhabited island" is unique in original editions of Shakespeare's plays; it is more like notes provided for the texts of court masques. Possibly scenery from earlier masques was utilized when the play was performed at court. But public performances would have been acted, as usual, before the unchanging facade of the playhouse interior.

The first scene on shipboard may have used ropes and tackle; possibly trap-doors served as hatches, and characters may have lept off stage as into the sea when the ship is said to "split."

The rest of the action is on the island which the text locates somewhere in the Mediterranean. Other allusions however, to the Bermudas and to the "plantation" of its land, indicate the New World; in the twentieth century, stage designers have borrowed from early drawings by Elizabethan settlers. Incidental references to flora and fauna are partly exotic and partly drawn from the English countryside. Some characters say the grass is "lush and lusty", others that the ground is tawny (II.i.51-52); there is talk of a "grove" of limetrees (V.i.10) and of "briers" and "furze" (IV.I.180), but at other times "no bush or shrub" is visible (II.ii.18).

Prospero's cell is on stage in V.i., with some means of revealing Ferdinand and Miranda playing chess together; I.ii and IV.i can be conveniently played in the same location, and possibly III.i. Act III, scene iii should have an upper level for Prospero to enter "on the top". (This would also be useful in I.i for the bridge of the ship.) The other scenes are played as if elsewhere on the island, being specifically *not* near Prospero's cell.

Note:
Where there is reason to believe that Shakespeare used a word in a very special or rare way, the gloss is marked with an asterisk.

captain   executive officer
(subordinate to the *master*)

what's to do

call to action   smartly

heartily
(to reduce drift to lee shore)
obey

1-7 Noise of the storm reverberates around the theater, lightning flashing from various places (see I.ii.198-208). Two men struggle onto the stage, shouting urgently above the storm or in its brief lulls. The Captain of the ship is then lost to sight. As the men hurry on and probably line up to be counted and receive orders, the Bosun takes command: hanging on for their lives, the sailors then start to climb or haul on ropes. The Master's whistle is heard again from offstage, but the next moment the Bosun's voice is cut off by a new burst of the storm. Probably all are still, grasping whatever they can, until the extreme

Blow till thou burst thy wind, if room enough!°

Enter ALONSO, SEBASTIAN, ANTONIO, FERDINAND, GONZALO, *and others.*

ALONSO   Good boatswain have care. Where's the master? Play
the men.°

BOATSWAIN   I pray now, keep below.   10

ANTONIO   Where is the master, bos'n?

BOATSWAIN   Do you not hear him? You mar our labor. Keep your
cabins; you do assist the storm.

GONZALO   Nay, good,° be patient.

BOATSWAIN   When the sea is. Hence! What cares these roarers° for 15
the name of king? To cabin! Silence! Trouble us not.

GONZALO   Good, yet remember whom thou hast aboard.

BOATSWAIN   None that I more love than myself. You are a councilor: if you can command these elements to silence, and
work° the peace of the present,° we will not hand a rope 20
more. Use your authority. If you cannot, give thanks you
have lived so long, and make yourself ready° in your cabin
for the mischance of the hour, if it so hap. Cheerly, good
hearts! Out of our way I say.   *Exit.*

GONZALO   I have great comfort from this fellow. Methinks he 25
hath no drowning mark upon him, his complexion° is per-
fect° gallows. Stand fast, good Fate, to his hanging! Make the
rope of his destiny° our cable, for our own doth little advantage.° If he be not born to be hanged,° our case is miserable.
                          Exit [with the other courtiers].

Enter BOATSWAIN.

BOATSWAIN   Down with topmast! Yare! Lower, lower! Bring her 30
to try with main course.°   *A cry within.*
A plague upon this howling! They are louder than the weather
or our office.°

let the storm blow itself out, if the ship's not too near shore

have courage

good fellow

rowdies (i.e., the waves)

bring about/handle (a ship)
this time (pun on royal *presence*)
i.e., say your prayers

appearance/nature
certain/sheer
i.e., hangman's rope/thread of life cut off by Fates
helps us little   (proverbial saying: "he that is born to be hanged will never be drowned")

lie hove-to with *try* (main) sail
The passengers make more noise than the storm or the mariners at their work.

violence is passed and the Bosun cries out, uselessly, at the wind (ll. 6-7).

So the play starts with instant clamor, violence and alarm, with skilled men working strenuously in great danger; a confused, yet necessarily disciplined, fragment of a scene.

8-29 The king and nobles, dressed as if for a wedding (see II.i.65-67), stumble on stage during another lull (perhaps through a trapdoor as if it were a hatch opening below deck). They are frightened, out of their element and therefore unusually helpless; they may well be sick. Separately their two leaders seek reassurance from the Bosun, asking for the absent Master who should be in charge.

The sailors continue to work at the ropes (l. 20), perhaps in response to the Master's whistle; but the Bosun may imply (l. 12) that their master is now the storm.

The Bosun's replies grow more insistent, forgetting ordinary servility and respect. But he takes time to reason with Gonzalo and then to mock him, after breaking off to rally his men (l. 23). Then he dismisses the more patient old councilor and the others with a curt order (ll. 23-24) which cares as little for "the name of king" as the storm does. He disappears from sight. Gonzalo tries to comfort the king or speaks for himself in a determinedly reasoned soliloquy; either way he is trying to face death and a sense of human impotence. By the time he is finished the storm has increased and everyone has scrambled for safety.

Sound and light effects can drown words in this scene, unless among all the various activity sufficient order is kept. Some directors create moments when everything is still and a single character or small group is picked out for attention by special lighting or positioning. The audience learns later that it is an artificial storm, so some unreality in the opening could be appropriate. The text indicates that loss of authority and hope must be as apparent as the terror of the storm.

30-45 The Bosun returns to cope with the growing storm, now acting without reference to the Master. As the sailors struggle at their work, a "cry within" adds a new, human and desperate sound to the storm.

Enter SEBASTIAN, ANTONIO, *and* GONZALO.

Yet again? What do you here? Shall we give o'er° and
drown? Have you a mind to sink?   35

SEBASTIAN   A pox o' your throat, you bawling, blasphemous,
incharitable dog!

BOATSWAIN   Work you, then.

ANTONIO   Hang, cur, hang, you whoreson, insolent noisemaker!
We are less afraid to be drowned than thou art.   40

GONZALO   I'll warrant him for drowning,° though the ship were
no stronger than a nutshell and as leaky as an unstanched°
wench.

BOATSWAIN   Lay her ahold,° ahold! Set her two courses° off to sea
again. Lay her off!°   45

Enter MARINERS *wet.*

MARINERS   All lost! To prayers, to prayers! All lost!   *[Exeunt.]*

BOATSWAIN   What, must our mouths be cold?°

GONZALO   The king and prince at prayers; let's assist them
For our case is as theirs.

SEBASTIAN   I am out of patience.

ANTONIO   We are merely° cheated of our lives by drunkards.   50
This wide-chopped° rascal—would thou mightst lie drowning
The washing of ten tides!°

GONZALO   He'll be hanged yet,
Though every drop of water swear against it
And gape at wid'st° to glut° him.
A confused noise within: "Mercy on us!"
"We split, we split!" "Farewell my wife and children!"   55
"Farewell brother!" "We split, we split, we split!"
                                                  [Exit BOATSWAIN.*]*

up

guarantee him against drowning

loose (lit., not watertight)
close to the wind   foresail
and mainsail

steer away from the shore

dead/without effect

utterly

open-mouthed/loud-mouthed

(pirates were hanged on shore
at low water, and kept there
for three tides)

desire most longingly/opens
its mouth the widest   feed
on/gulp down

Three courtiers enter, beginning to be "infected"
in their reason and playing "tricks of desperation (see
I.ii.209-12); they are probably ready to abandon ship.
Gonzalo keeps some sense of humor but his wit is
cruder. Sebastian's comments (and Gonzalo's at
V.i.218-20) suggest that Shakespeare wrote more
violent oaths for the Bosun only to have them cen-
sored for print. The words he is given are more blunt
in dismissing his passengers, precise and detailed in
giving orders to the men. After line 43 it seems that
the storm has yet greater violence; the sailors actions
become more urgent and less constant.

46-47 More sailors enter, as if just drenched by the
great sea. They obey no orders, but panic, running
offstage almost at once. The others all follow, disci-
pline giving way as each thinks of his own safety.
Line 51 suggests that the Bosun remains on stage a
little longer, but his last speech implies that he goes
off to rouse the men to fresh effort; Ariel says later
that they all remained on the ship (I.ii.212-13).

48-60 The courtiers hang together for a moment as
the stage empties: Gonzalo giving up hope of survival, Sebastian asserting his desperation, and
Antonio cursing others, furious at his own lack of
resource—all highly uncharacteristic reactions.
At line 54 there is a noise—more appalling than
any before—which includes the sound of wrenching
timber and cries of horror (some of which are speci-
fied in the text). Probably the Bosun should continue
to give orders and to swear, but everyone seems to
go "mad" (see I.ii.209-17). The ship should seem to
be "afire" and the courtiers reckless, terrified and
doomed. Instinctively, Antonio and Sebastian run to
rejoin the king's center of operations.

ANTONIO   Let's all sink wi' th' king.

SEBASTIAN   Let's take leave of him.
                                             Exit [with ANTONIO].

GONZALO   Now would I give a thousand furlongs of sea for an acre
    of barren ground—long heath,° brown furze° anything.
    The wills above be done, but I would fain die a dry death.   60
                                                          Exit.

Scene ii *Enter* PROSPERO *and* MIRANDA.

MIRANDA   If by your art,° my dearest father, you have
    Put the wild waters in this roar, allay them.
    The sky, it seems, would pour down stinking pitch,
    But that the sea, mounting to th' welkin's cheek,°
    Dashes the fire out. O, I have suffered   5
    With those that I saw suffer! A brave° vessel,
    Who had no doubt some noble creature in her,
    Dashed all to pieces. O the cry did knock
    Against my very heart. Poor souls, they perished.
    Had I been any god of power, I would   10
    Have sunk the sea within the earth, or ere°
    It should the good ship so have swallowed and
    The fraughting° souls within her.

PROSPERO   Be collected;°
    No more amazement.° Tell your piteous° heart
    There's no harm done.

MIRANDA   O woe the day!

PROSPERO   No harm.   15
    I have done nothing but in care of thee,
    Of thee my dear one, thee my daughter, who
    Art ignorant of what thou art, naught knowing
    Of whence I am, nor that I am more better
    Than Prospero, master of a full° poor cell,   20
    And thy no greater father.

MIRANDA   More to know
    Did never meddle with my thoughts.°

heather   gorse

By line 58 Gonzalo is alone onstage. His last speech is effective if said, while the storm is briefly quiet, as a prayer, or as a flash of clear consciousness before facing death by drowning. His whole body will be tense as he finds something to clutch hold of to steady himself, and his voice, therefore, strained and intense. The contrast with other speeches, especially in the enumeration of the kinds of "barren ground" and in the attempts at humor, can make a pathetic or a courageous impression.

magical power

face of the sky

fine

1-13   As noise of the storm continues offstage (at least until l. 5), Prospero is seen silent and probably quite still. (In Jacobean theaters he was probably "discovered" by drawing back a curtain from an inner or upper part of the stage.) The contrast with the frightened mariners and courtiers is extreme. He may hold his magic staff in outstretched hand, in charge of the tempest and then of the new silence.

before

conveyed as freight

composed
bewildered/terror   pitying

The storm, however, is echoed in Miranda's words and her tears (see l. 25). Prospero does not reply to "my dearest father" and so she may turn away and the rest of her speech be a soliloquy. Certainly she is torn by contrary reactions, changing from trying to understand what she sees and what she imagines, to direct expression of her own suffering and her sympathy for others. Her thoughts settle (as more sustained rhythm and syntax indicate) only when she realizes what she would have done had she possessed the power of a "god." The audience, still knowing little of the situation, may sense that Prospero, clothed in his magic robe, is indeed a "god of power", and implacable.

exceedingly

enter my mind, trouble my mind

13-25   Prospero speaks first in short phrases, suggesting that he is still preoccupied with controlling the storm; his affection for Miranda becomes clear only when she continues to cry (see l. 15). But now he speaks only in riddles, which are either stiffened with pride or softened with self-deprecating humor; either way, or with a touch of both, Miranda learns little new.

The trust and innocence of her next reply (ll. 21-22) prompts his "'Tis time...." (the word itself placed strongly at the completion of her verse-line), the first of many references to crucial timing (see also ll. 36-37).

Probably Prospero still does not move, or he retires from the upper stage to reappear below.

PROSPERO   'Tis time
　　I should inform thee farther. Lend thy hand
　　And pluck my magic garment from me.—So,
                                          [Lays down his robe.]
　　Lie there, my art. Wipe thou thine eyes; have comfort.   25
　　The direful spectacle of the wreck, which touched
　　The very virtue° of compassion in thee,
　　I have with such provision° in mine art
　　So safely ordered that there is no soul . . .
　　No, not so much perdition° as an hair   30
　　Betid° to any creature in the vessel
　　Which thou heard'st cry, which thou saw'st sink. Sit down,
　　For thou must now know farther.

MIRANDA   You have often
　　Begun to tell me what I am, but stopped
　　And left me to a bootless inquisition,°   35
　　Concluding, "Stay; not yet."

PROSPERO   The hour's now come;
　　The very minute bids thee ope thine ear.
　　Obey, and be attentive.
　　Canst thou remember
　　A time before we came unto this cell?   40
　　I do not think thou canst, for then thou wast not
　　Out° three years old.

MIRANDA   Certainly sir, I can.

PROSPERO   By what? By any other house or person?
　　Of anything the image,° tell me, that
　　Hath kept with thy remembrance.

MIRANDA   'Tis far off,   45
　　And rather like a dream than an assurance°
　　That my remembrance warrants. Had I not
　　Four or five women once that tended me?

PROSPERO   Thou hadst, and more, Miranda. But how is it
　　That this lives in thy mind? What seest thou else   50
　　In the dark backward° and abysm° of time?
　　If thou rememb'rest aught ere thou cam'st here,
　　How thou cam'st here thou mayst.

Miranda approaches him to help with the disrobing—
a ritual action, perhaps accompanied with music.
Usually the robe is heavy and decorated with hiero-
glyphics. Once this is laid aside, Prospero could take
Miranda in his arms; he looks into her eyes (see l. 25)
and comforts her; he has changed from a godlike figure to a father. But he is not yet completely intimate:
the address to his "art" could be formal and he does
not "wipe" her eyes for her; his speech is economical
and short-phrased.

essence

foresight/preparation

loss (pun: *perdition* = damna-
tion)

befallen

26-53 Now Prospero speaks with considerate reassurance; the phrasing is sustained over several lines.
He echoes Miranda's very first words—"If by your
art,..."—and her instinctive cry—"Poor souls, they
perished"—and her "creature" and "vessel": clearly
he had been more attentive than he had shown. At
the end of line 29, however, Prospero stops abruptly,
momentarily losing his train of thought as he remembers the evil (see the pun on "perdition") wrought by

fruitless inquiry

his treacherous brother. This adds a strangeness to
his exposition, for the audience, like Miranda, still
knows almost nothing of the situation. Although
asked to "sit down" at line 32, Miranda does not do so
until line 38. Prospero, aware of the "very minute" of
a crisis, waits, nevertheless, until he is sure of her full
attention and then, after pausing, he asks a question,
to which he supplies a partial answer himself, so
betraying his own anxiety.

In the twelve years they have been alone
together, he has never spoken before of his earlier

quite

life. To him the past is, for the most part, "dark" (l.
51), hateful and dangerous (see "abysm"); Miranda
responds to his mood and, while answering "certainly" at first, describes her remembrance only in the
form of a question. The father is preparing carefully

mental picture

to dismantle a barrier between his thoughts and his
child's; gently and apprehensively he is gauging her
mind so that she can hear what she must be told if
the crisis is to be faced and resolved.

certainty

Probably Prospero remains standing with
Miranda sitting at his feet. He may walk restlessly
about and remain alert to what is happening elsewhere on the island or the sea, or in the sky. They
cannot be very intimate, sitting down together for
example, because Miranda does not answer any of
Prospero's questions straightaway; twice he asks
two questions together (ll. 43 and 49-51).

past   chasm

MIRANDA   But that I do not.

PROSPERO   Twelve year since, Miranda, twelve year since,°
Thy father was the Duke of Milan and   55
A prince of power.

MIRANDA   Sir, are not you my father?

PROSPERO   Thy mother was a piece° of virtue, and
She said thou wast my daughter; and thy father
Was Duke of Milan, and his only heir,
And princess, no worse issued.°

MIRANDA   O the heavens!   60
What foul play had we, that we came from thence?
Or blessèd was't we did?

PROSPERO   Both, both my girl!
By foul play, as thou say'st, were we heaved° thence,
But blessedly holp° hither.

MIRANDA   O my heart bleeds
To think o' th' teen° that I have turned you to,   65
Which is from° my remembrance! Please you, farther.

PROSPERO   My brother and thy uncle, called Antonio—
I pray thee mark me, that a brother should
Be so perfidious!—he whom next thyself
Of all the world I loved, and to him put   70
The manage° of my state, as at that time
Through all the signories° it was the first,°
And Prospero the prime duke, being so reputed
In dignity, and for the liberal arts°
Without a parallel. Those being all my study,   75
The government I cast° upon my brother,
And to my state grew stranger,° being transported
And rapt in secret° studies. Thy false uncle—
Dost thou attend me?

MIRANDA   Sir, most heedfully.

PROSPERO   Being once perfected° how to grant suits,°   80
How to deny them, who t' advance, and who
To trash for overtopping,° new-created
The creatures that were mine, I say—or° changed 'em,

ago

perfect example/woman (usually derogatory)

no humbler in birth

removed, forced

helped

anxiety

out of

administration

states (of Italy)　supreme

humane learning

got rid of, shed

withdrew from public life and duties

occult/private

having once mastered　petitions

check (hunting term) for getting above themselves*

either

54-56 Prospero now reveals the central fact in simple and impressive words. His sense of "high wrongs" (see V.i.25) and his determination to right them may be suggested by the repetition in line 54. Miranda's reply can be confused, disbelieving or, even, reproving.

57-60 Prospero jokes (and may laugh) to allay Miranda's anxiety, and then starts to recount the salient facts once more. He has yet to tell the worst of his story and so may take her in arms as he speaks of her teasingly as of a third person.

61-79 After her instinctive exclamation, Miranda's double question shows her to be confident of her father's goodness, optimistically hopeful and eager to be taught: her innocence and affection will shine through her anxiety.

Prospero responds with quick reassurance and the more tender "my girl." But to Miranda's heartfelt response (ll. 64-66) he says nothing until she specifically requests him to proceed. His heart and mind are both so full that he approaches the heart of the matter with reluctance but, once started, with emphatic energy. He may stand a little apart, tense and absorbed, his eyes seldom looking towards Miranda now.

The parenthesis of lines 68-69 indicates a moment of direct contact, but stern and corrective rather than affectionate. His difficulty in re-living the past is further expressed by elaborate syntax, displaced phrases, reference to himself as Prospero. The sudden turning to Miranda at line 79 may imply that he knows he has been carried away by his sense of wrong and betrayal; or he may now be walking to and fro to control his passion and is suddenly recalled to the purpose of his tale only by seeing Miranda. Alternatively his mind is working with great speed and he includes his daughter swiftly, to make sure she is able to follow. In any case, his question signifies that there is now some distance between them.

80-89 Assured of Miranda's attention, Prospero now speaks directly of his brother and other traitors: he chooses his words with care and active imagination, at lines 83-84 halting the forward impulse to correct and amplify what he has said. When he speaks again

Or else new-formed 'em—having both the key°
Of officer and office, set all hearts i' th' state   85
To what tune pleased his ear; that now he was
The ivy which had hid my princely trunk
And sucked my verdure° out on't.—Thou attend'st not?

MIRANDA   O good sir, I do.

PROSPERO   I pray thee mark me.—
I thus neglecting worldly ends, all dedicated   90
To closeness° and the bettering of my mind
With that which, but by being so retired,
O'erprized all popular rate,° in my false brother
Awaked an evil nature; and my trust,
Like a good parent, did beget° of him   95
A falsehood in its contrary as great
As my trust was, which had indeed no limit,
A confidence sans° bound. He being thus lorded,°
Not only with what my revenue yielded
But what my power might else exact, like one   100
Who having into truth, by telling of it,
Made such a sinner of his memory
To credit his own lie,° he did believe
He was indeed the duke, out o' th' substitution°
And executing th' outward face of royalty   105
With all prerogative.°
Hence his ambition growing—Dost thou hear?

MIRANDA   Your tale, sir, would cure deafness.

PROSPERO   To have no screen° between this part he played
And him he played it for, he needs will be   110
Absolute Milan.° Me, poor man, my library
Was dukedom large enough. Of temporal royalties°
He thinks me now incapable; confederates—
So dry he was for sway°—wi' th' King of Naples
To give him annual tribute, do him homage,   115
Subject his coronet to his crown, and bend
The dukedom, yet unbowed—alas, poor Milan!—
To most ignoble stooping.°

MIRANDA   O the heavens!

control/musical key

i.e., power

seclusion

public, ordinary consideration

(proverbial saying: "trust is the mother of deceit")

without   made a lord

who lies so constantly that he believes his own lie and so sins further against truth (*into* = unto; *to* = as to)
in consequence of being my deputy
rights and privileges

division

Duke of Milan in fact
worldly royal duties

he was so greedy for power

humiliation

of himself, his feelings are expressed in images of growth, strength and slow physical torture. He turns once more to Miranda; she may have sunk her head into her hands, suffering with what she hears (compare I.ii.5-6). John Gielgud played this scene as "still an angry man" who has achieved control over his reactions only with difficulty: "he has not eliminated passion; he has mastered it...You cannot take your eyes off him as one strong emotion succeeds another in that lined, expressive, mobile countenance:...he is living and suffering the experience as he narrates it" (*Shakespeare Quarterly*, 8 (1957), 488-89).

90-109   Prospero goes back to the beginning of his tale, longer phrasing suggesting a slower pace. But complicated syntax and word-order (the initial "I" governing the main verb, "Awaked", four lines later), with second thoughts and explanations, all suggest care and deliberation: he is retelling the story so that all possible blame is placed on his own actions—it is his "trust" which awoke "evil."

As thoughts of Antonio's treachery possess his mind (l. 106), the incomplete verse-line suggests that he stops, his unspoken thoughts occupying his mind. Perhaps he thinks now of his own prerogative gained by a more than royal art—his power, already manifested in the tempest, by which he will exact revenge and restitution. But starting once more, he breaks off to turn more gently to Miranda (contrast ll. 88-89), as if to prove that he is in control of all elements of his tale. He pauses briefly again after his daughter's reply (note the incomplete line), but continues without break in his sense; he has almost bridged the gap which was between them.

110-40   Having named Antonio's ambition to be "Absolute Milan," Prospero once more becomes impassioned, expressing his thoughts with sarcastic irony and then a fourfold reiteration of the ignominious price Antonio paid for power. His rhetorical build-up is broken, however, by an instinctive "alas, poor Milan," which is echoed by Miranda's less specific exclamation (l. 118). He responds to her concern by asking her to judge rationally, insisting that she know the precise terms of his princedom's subjugation.

Miranda, brought up on an almost uninhabited island, is out of her depth: the nearest she can get to imagining the situation is to consider her grandmoth-

PROSPERO   Mark his condition,° and th' event;° then tell me
    If this might be a brother.

MIRANDA   I should sin   120
    To think but° nobly of my grandmother;
    Good wombs have borne bad sons.

PROSPERO   Now the condition:
    This King of Naples, being an enemy
    To me inveterate, hearkens my brother's suit,
    Which was, that he, in lieu o' th' premises°   125
    Of homage, and I know not how much tribute,
    Should presently° extirpate me and mine
    Out of the dukedom, and confer fair Milan,
    With all the honors, on my brother. Whereon,
    A treacherous army levied, one midnight   130
    Fated to th' purpose, did Antonio open
    The gates of Milan; and i' th' dead of darkness,
    The ministers° for th' purpose hurried thence
    Me and thy crying self.

MIRANDA   Alack, for pity!
    I, not rememb'ring how I cried out then,   135
    Will cry it o'er again; it is a hint°
    That wrings° mine eyes to't.

PROSPERO   Hear a little further,
    And then I'll bring thee to the present business
    Which now's upon's; without the which, this story
    Were most impertinent.°

MIRANDA   Wherefore did they not   140
    That hour destroy us?

PROSPERO   Well demanded, wench.
    My tale provokes that question. Dear, they durst not,
    So dear the love my people bore me; nor set
    A mark so bloody° on the business; but,
    With colors° fairer, painted their foul ends.   145
    In few,° they hurried us aboard a bark,
    Bore us some leagues to sea, where they prepared
    A rotten carcass of a butt,° not rigged,
    Nor tackle, sail, nor mast; the very rats

agreement, treaty   consequence

other than

in return for guarantees

immediately

agents

occasion
forces

pointless

(as hunters were *blooded* after
   killing a deer)

false appearances
briefly
tub

er and what she has been told about family histories.
Prospero presses on without comment and starts to
recall the *coup d'état* more calmly.

From political issues, Prospero is drawn back
into the actual drama of the particular night, investing
it with hellish images as well as a sense of immediacy. With "Me and thy crying self," a new reality and
feeling comes into his speech, a recollection of a
young child's helplessness and of a tenderness that
has outlasted the catastrophe. Miranda now weeps
openly and can speak further only of her own inade-
quacy. This may well be the moment when Prospero
sits down beside his daughter (he has taken this
position by line 171); he continues more gently,
explaining that she must still be patient and attentive.
He is also aware once more that time presses: he
knows, throughout this difficult narration, that a crisis
is upon him (see ll. 138-39). For this reason, perhaps, he had tried to tell her too much too soon
(compare Miranda's misunderstanding at line 56),
pressed her with questions earlier still (ll. 40, 43, 50-
51), eagerly seized on what she understood (see
"Both, both..", l. 62), constantly asked her to pay strict
attention, and here seems to cut her off with "Now the
condition" (l. 122).

140-45 Miranda's question shows that she is now
more secure in her father's attention and presence.
Prospero seems surprised momentarily by her grasp
of the situation, but he is more affectionate (see
"wench" and "Dear" ll. 141, 142); he proceeds more
calmly with his tale and remembers "the love my people bore me."

(Antonio's decision to cast Prospero and
Miranda adrift in a boat is the stuff of romantic fiction
rather than political reality. By arranging the exposition so that Miranda's puzzlement is answered in a
moment of mutual confidence and growing signs of
affection, Shakespeare encourages a more ready
acceptance of this circumstance by the theatre audience; it is pleased to follow where Miranda leads.)

146-60 As he tells of their ordeal in the open boat,
Prospero re-lives the scene in his imagination. The
rhythms of his speech and its imagery suggest that
he is at first bitter, but then grows quieter and more
reflective, turning the very sea and winds into active

Instinctively have quit it. There they hoist° us,   150
To cry to th' sea that roared to us, to sigh
To th' winds whose pity, sighing back again,
Did us but loving wrong.°

MIRANDA   Alack, what trouble
Was I then to you!

PROSPERO   O, a cherubin
Thou wast that did preserve me! Thou didst smile,   155
Infusèd° with a fortitude from heaven—
When I have decked° the sea with drops full salt,°
Under my burden° groaned—which raised in me
An undergoing stomach,° to bear up°
Against what should ensue.

MIRANDA   How came we ashore?   160

PROSPERO   By providence divine.
Some food we had, and some fresh water, that
A noble Neapolitan, Gonzalo,
Out of his charity, who being then appointed
Master of this design,° did give us, with   165
Rich garments, linens, stuffs, and necessaries
Which since have steaded° much. So, of his gentleness,°
Knowing I loved my books, he furnished me
From mine own library with volumes that
I prize above my dukedom.

MIRANDA   Would I might   170
But ever° see that man.

PROSPERO   Now I arise.
Sit still,° and hear the last of our sea sorrow.
Here in this island we arrived, and here
Have I, thy schoolmaster, made thee more profit°
Than other princess° can, that have more time   175
For vainer° hours, and tutors not so careful.

MIRANDA   Heavens thank you for't. And now I pray you, sir—
For still 'tis beating in my mind—your reason
For raising this sea storm?

cast off

i.e., the winds blew only in
sympathy with the fugi-
tives' sighs

inspired

covered (puns: *decked* =
adorned; *deck* of a ship)
i.e., tears

(puns: *burden* = freight of ship;
burden = refrain of song)

sustaining courage   keep
going/bring ship into the
wind

enterprise, plot

been of use   noble qualities

some day

continue to sit

make progress
princesses
more foolish

sympathizers. Miranda's interjections (at ll. 153-54)
draws him forward in the tale and awakens an even
more powerful memory of innocence and instinctive
trust. (The image is complicated and precise,
because cherubims were associated with God's
presence in the winds, and with endless patience
and endurance.) Under this influence, Prospero sees
his past afflictions more objectively (see ll. 157-60);
Miranda's simple question (l. 160) suggests that she
is growing still closer to her father and is more at
ease with his story.

161   An incomplete verse-line indicates that this
short reply is followed by a mutual silence: Prospero
is mindful of a power greater than himself—later he
calls it "Fortune" (i.ii.180) and "Mercy itself" (see
Epilogue, l. 18).

162-86 Prospero speaks freely of his friend, but the
syntax is still not altogether simple. As Miranda
responds to this more outgoing mood, Prospero
changes abruptly (l. 171) and stands up: he probably
moves away from her, before resuming the story. At
line 172 he may again put on his magic robe (see ll.
24-25) so awakening the audience's expectation and
Miranda's, and accentuating the authority of his following words.
    Miranda is, however, newly confident and
repeats her question about the storm (ll. 177-79); she
may have forgotten his order to "sit still" (l. 172) and
risen to move closer to his side. He reasserts his
authority, alluding to his own supernatural powers as
"prescience" (l. 182) and telling what is to happen
only in most general terms. He is now thinking of his
moment for taking revenge on his "enemies" (l. 181)
and stops her "questions" (l. 186); he has not directly answered her pressing enquiry about his reason
for raising the storm (l. 178-79).
    Again Prospero is alert and aware of the exact
moment for action; see "now" (ll. 171, 181, 185) and
"more time For vainer hours...." (ll. 175-76). Again he
may look offstage to where his enemies may be coming shore, or above the stage towards the stars painted on the "heavens" over the stage of a Jacobean
theater.

PROSPERO   Know thus far forth:
By accident most strange, bountiful Fortune,   180
Now my dear lady,° hath mine enemies
Brought to this shore; and by my prescience
I find my zenith° doth depend upon
A most auspicious star, whose influence°
If now I court not, but omit,° my fortunes   185
Will ever after droop. Here cease more questions.
Thou art inclined to sleep: 'tis a good dullness,
And give it way.° I know thou canst not choose.
                              [MIRANDA sleeps.]
Come away,° servant, come! I am ready now.
Approach, my Ariel! Come!   190

                        Enter ARIEL.

ARIEL   All hail, great master! Grave° sir, hail! I come
To answer thy best pleasure, be't to fly,
To swim, to dive into the fire, to ride
On the curled clouds. To thy strong bidding task°
Ariel, and all his quality.°

PROSPERO   Hast thou, spirit,   195
Performed to point° the tempest that I bade thee?

ARIEL   To every article.
I boarded the king's ship: now on the beak,°
Now in the waist, the deck,° in every cabin,
I flamed amazement.° Sometime I'd divide   200
And burn in many places; on the topmast,
The yards, and boresprit° would I flame distinctly,°
Then meet and join. Jove's lightnings, the precursors
O' th' dreadful thunderclaps, more momentary
And sight-outrunning were not. The fire and cracks   205
Of sulfurous roaring the most mighty Neptune
Seem to besiege, and make his bold waves tremble,
Yea, his dread trident shake.

PROSPERO   My brave° spirit!
Who was so firm, so constant, that this coil°
Would not infect his reason?

patroness (not whore or foe)

highest point of fortune

astral power

neglect

scope

come here

respected

put to the proof

fellow spirits/powers

in every detail

pointed prow

poop

awoke terror by appearing as fire

bowsprit   separately

fine

turmoil

187-90   The first magic the audience sees Prospero actually perform puts Miranda to sleep in a moment, exactly when he chooses. He may hold his magic staff over her; music may be heard. Use of his power separates Prospero totally from his daughter and raises many issues about its purpose that have been held back by the preceding duologue. In effect Prospero is now alone, and Miranda powerless and inert, her growing confidence extinguished.

Immediately a further surprise follows: Prospero speaks, as a matter of usual occurrence, to the air. He need not move; his authority is complete and his power implicit in curt phrases. But again he is aware of time: "I am ready *now*" (l. 189).

191-97   Ariel's first line is ceremonious, yet playful with its echoing vowel-sounds: it could be spoken off-stage, as if it were sounds in the wind. In contrast his offer of service is energetic; actors often speak the active verbs expressively, like a verbal dance.

In some productions, Ariel flies on or descends from above, demonstrating his unhuman kinship with air; he may hover close to Prospero's head, not touching ground. He may dance on, or his voice may be heard, from all around and above the stage, before his entrance. His reference to "all his quality" (l. 195) has been taken as cue to bring a group of fellow spirits on stage with him; however it is not easy to find tasks for them in this scene.

Prospero's question about the "tempest" provides helpful exposition for the audience. Ariel's first short answer (l. 197) accentuates his quick, complete obedience and Prospero's power as "master." In a following pause, Prospero will seem to wait for, and so command, further information.

198-208   The rhythms of Ariel's narrative are alert and quick at first, but lengthen, probably in pleasure, as he describes the horror he has caused. He ends, in the present tense, with a sense of immediacy; there is pride and amusement, or laughter, here.

Most Ariels mime or illustrate the events they describe: this gives an arresting impression to the spirit's first appearance; it also varies and enlivens the long exposition that Shakespeare's choice of a short time-span for the play's action has necessitated.

208-17   Although quick to show his pleasure to Ariel, Prospero reflects on the awful effects of the tempest he has raised, either delighting in the torture he inflicts or remembering his own sufferings. It is prob-

ARIEL   Not a soul   210
But felt a fever of the mad° and played
Some tricks of desperation.° All but mariners
Plunged in the foaming brine and quit the vessel,
Then all afire with me. The king's son Ferdinand,
With hair up-staring°—then like reeds, not hair—   215
Was the first man that leapt; cried, "Hell is empty,
And all the devils are here!"

PROSPERO   Why, that's my spirit!
But was not this nigh shore?

ARIEL   Close by, my master.

PROSPERO   But are they, Ariel, safe?   *Keeps them unharmed*

ARIEL   Not a hair perished:
On their sustaining garments not a blemish,   220
But fresher than before; and as thou bad'st me,
In troops I have dispersed them 'bout the isle.
The king's son have I landed by himself,
Whom I left cooling of the air with sighs
In an odd angle° of the isle, and sitting,   225
His arms in this sad knot.   *[Illustrates with a gesture.]*

PROSPERO   Of the king's ship,
The mariners, say how thou hast disposed,
And all the rest o' th' fleet.

ARIEL   Safely in harbor
Is the king's ship, in the deep nook where once
Thou call'dst me up at midnight to fetch dew°   230
From the still-vexed° Bermoothes,° there she's hid;
The mariners all under hatches stowed,
Who, with a charm joined to their suff'red° labor,
I have left asleep. And for the rest o' th' fleet,
Which I dispersed, they all have met again,   235
And are upon the Mediterranean float°
Bound sadly home for Naples,
Supposing that they saw the king's ship wrecked
And his great person perish.   *Believe the king is dead*

like madmen feel
strange reckless actions

standing on end

out-of-the-way corner

(used in magic; see line 323)
always stormy*   Bermudas

inflicted

sea

ably the former, because Ariel continues brightly: he is not "human" and so does not sympathize with "tricks of desperation" in men; he may laugh or speak with mock sadness. Ferdinand's cry is, for Ariel, proof of his own adroitness; it is spoken in pride or with laughter, or with a consummate impression of high drama and seriousness, undercut by exaggeration.

Prospero's "that's my spirit" (l. 217) identifies him with Ariel's achievement, even more closely than "my brave spirit" (l. 208); these short phrases cap Ariel's much longer ones and so imply some controlling power as well as approval or pleasure. Prospero follows now with a precise question, to which Ariel replies just as precisely, acknowledging his (enforced) subservience. Throughout the play, the actors of these two parts are able to respond with great subtlety to each other's performance, the effect heightened by the quick changes of mood and rhythm that they share.

219-26 When Prospero checks on the safety of the court party, Ariels offers more detail than necessary; he speaks as if quoting from Prospero's charge to him. He may be reflecting Prospero's particular concern when he proceeds, unasked, to speak again of Ferdinand. However his amused mimicry of the prince's silent expression of grief raises no response.

226-39 There may be some impatience in the phrasing of Prospero's question, but Ariel is now relaxed, making light of difficulties and confident of approval. His recollection of employment in the "still-vexed Bermoothes" (l. 231) associates Prospero's magic with the New World which was being newly discovered and exploited in Shakespeare's day and a theme for wonder and for cupidity. But his reference to "midnight" and "dew" also brings associations with sorcery, such as Medea's (see *Merchant of Venice*, V.i.6-14), and with the world of fairies (as in *Midsummer Night's Dream*). So this passage deepens the audience's understanding and quickens its imagination. The short line 237 may indicate a pause for approval on reaching the last charge Prospero had given him, or for further laughter at suffering.

PROSPERO   Ariel, thy charge
Exactly is performed; but there's more work.   240
What is the time o' th' day?

ARIEL   Past the mid season.°

PROSPERO   At least two glasses.° The time 'twixt six and now
Must by us both be spent most preciously.

ARIEL   Is there more toil? Since thou dost give me pains,°
Let me remember thee what thou hast promised,   245
Which is not yet performed me.

PROSPERO   How now? Moody?°
What is't thou canst demand?

ARIEL   My liberty.

PROSPERO   Before the time be out? No more!

ARIEL   I prithee,
Remember I have done thee worthy service,
Told thee no lies, made thee no mistakings,° served   250
Without or grudge or grumblings. Thou did promise
To bate me° a full year.

PROSPERO   Dost thou forget
From what a torment I did free thee?

ARIEL   No.

PROSPERO   Thou dost; and think'st it much° to tread the ooze
Of the salt deep. . .   255
To run upon the sharp wind of the North,
To do me business in the veins° o' th' earth
When it is baked° with frost.

ARIEL   I do not sir.

PROSPERO   Thou liest, malignant° thing. Hast thou forgot
The foul witch Sycorax, who with age and envy°   260
Was grown into a hoop? Hast thou forgot her?

ARIEL   No, sir.

PROSPERO   Thou hast. Where was she born? Speak! Tell me.

ARIEL   Sir, in Argier.°

noon

hour-glasses (i.e., two o'clock)

toil/punishment

sullen, headstrong

mistakes

let me off

art reluctant

i.e., watercourses
hardened

rebellious/noxious
ill will

Algiers

239-43 Prospero becomes more severe, concerned with the next stage of his plan: his praise is curt, his warning of "more work" terse. Again he is alert to the exact time (see note, ll. 13-25), correcting Ariel's imprecision; but now his mind travels ahead.

Prospero sees Ariel and himself working "both" (l. 243) to the same purpose: however active and free to move Ariel has been during his report, the master will now be close to the servant, as the man takes charge of the spirit.

244-47 Ariel changes immediately: his question is direct and his protest firm. Yet when challenged by Prospero, Ariel's simple, far-ranging reply is still more surprising. "My liberty" springs from a depth of his being not expressed before. In performance, the cry can be prolonged in anguish, tense and vibrant with frustration, or musically alive, as if, even in servitude, Ariels responds with instinctive pleasure to the very idea of freedom. He may tremble in frenzy or stand stone-still in defiance.

248-95 Prospero's repressive "No more!" can be as surprising as Ariel's cry for liberty. When the servant pleads "worthy service", truth and politeness, and when he reminds his master of a promise, Prospero over-rides him. Ariel's "No" (l. 253) can sound cowed or still rebellious; usually, he cringes expecting an immediate return of punishment. ("Once in a month", Prospero has reminded him of past suffering in order to enforce obedience; see l. 264.). When Prospero continues, Ariel's replies are brief and probably frightened; he addresses his master submissively as "sir" (ll. 258, 262, 263, 270), as he has not since his first dignified "Grave sir" (l. 191).

At line 262, Ariel delays answering, and when he does say what his master expects, he is rewarded with sarcasm. At line 270, when Ariel gives an immediate answer, Prospero waits without comment before proceeding. Prospero seems to be punishing a "malignant thing" (l. 259), or training Ariel as if he were a dog to be taught to heel and respond to routine orders.

If Ariel does indeed "cleave" to Prospero's thoughts (see IV.i.165), responding totally and quickly to whatever his master wills, this recapitulation will cause him to suffer. He will wince as Prospero details hard service (ll. 254-58); he may experience some relief when told about Sycorax, but will fear what is coming—a total recall of the confinement he had suffered at her hands. At lines 282-83, Ariel may fall at Prospero's feet, "imprisoned" and convulsed, his "groans" once more cleaving the stillness command-

PROSPERO   O, was she so? I must
Once in a month recount what thou hast been,
Which thou forget'st. This damned witch Sycorax,   265
For mischiefs° manifold, and sorceries terrible
To enter human hearing, from Argier,
Thou know'st was banished. For one thing she did
They would not take her life. Is not this true?

ARIEL   Ay, sir.   270

PROSPERO   This blue-eyed° hag was hither brought with child
And here was left by th' sailors. Thou, my slave,
As thou report'st thyself, wast then her servant;
And for° thou wast a spirit too delicate°
To act her earthy and abhorred commands,   275
Refusing her grand hests,° she did confine thee,
By help of her more potent ministers,°
And in her most unmitigable rage,
Into a cloven pine; within which rift
Imprisoned, thou didst painfully remain   280
A dozen years; within which space she died
And left thee there, where thou didst vent thy groans
As fast as millwheels strike. Then was this island—
Save for the son that she did litter° here,
A freckled whelp, hagborn—not honored with   285
A human shape.

ARIEL   Yes: Caliban her son.

PROSPERO   Dull° thing, I say so! He, that Caliban
Whom now I keep in service. Thou best know'st
What torment I did find thee in; thy groans
Did make wolves howl and penetrate the breasts°   290
Of ever-angry bears. It was a torment
To lay upon the damned, which Sycorax
Could not again undo. It was mine art,
When I arrived and heard thee, that made gape
The pine, and let thee out.

ARIEL   I thank thee master.   295

PROSPERO   If thou more murmur'st, I will rend an oak
And peg thee in his° knotty entrails, till

evil deeds

(the color of eyelids was regarded as a sign of pregnancy)

because   finely sensitive

commands

agents

bring forth (normally said of animals)

obtuse, tedious

touch the hearts

its

ed by Prospero. He seems eager to get his master to talk of Caliban rather than himself (see I. 286), but immediately Prospero tightens the noose around Ariel's thoughts. As soon as Prospero speaks of his deliverance, Ariel's thanks are fully submissive (see I. 295).

Much depends on how Prospero leads Ariel through this recital of torment. He can express sympathy or regret, but this is held in check by the remorseless forward pressure of the verse once he has started: he hesitates at line 255, but not after "Thou liest" (I. 259); then the narrative also presses forward. From "Thou, my slave" (I. 272) a single sentence is sustained until Prospero reaches the energy of Ariel's "groans" at line 283. In performance Prospero usually seems to be harshly repressive or even cruel. However played, this is very different from the Prospero seen with Miranda—self-critical, passionate but also deeply sensitive, at times affectionate or humorous. He can still be witty, but severely so. He is terse, emphatic, impatient, bullying perhaps. Strong feeling, however, causes him to reveal further reaches in his imagination: Ariel's missions awake keen responses to the pain inflicted by nature (see II. 254-58); Sycorax's hooped body is like a figure from Dante's *Inferno* (see II. 260-61); Ariel's suffering evokes the noise and resistless pressure of "mill-wheels" (I. 283) and his "groans" the howling of "wolves" and unthinking stubbornness of "bears" (II. 290, 291); finally a split "pine" is seen to "gape" as if it were a human mouth or wound (I. 294). Thus, at his most repressive, Prospero is also alive to sensuous experience and so draws an audience into his thoughts, no matter how painfully Ariel suffers. He finishes by opposing his "art" to the "torment" of the "damned", and so awakens thoughts of a Christian theology and at the same time assumes the role of a "god of power" (see I. 10, above). The exertion needed to speak these speeches, with their powerful, compact imagery, agile syntax and varying rhythms, makes very apparent in performance how strongly Prospero is committed to this encounter with his "airy" spirit.

296-302   Prospero answers Ariel's submissive thanks with threat of still greater and longer torment, expressed in compact, physical language as "knotted" as the oak itself. Ariel probably kneels as he asks, with utmost simplicity, for pardon; and without waiting for reply, he offers obedience and service. He is accepted and with a word of hope and so, like a spring released, he is on his feet again, or in the air, his whole being now quick and free. His brisk and

Thou hast howled away twelve winters.

ARIEL   Pardon, master,
  I will be correspondent° to command
  And do my spriting° gently.

PROSPERO   Do so; and after two days   300
  I will discharge thee.

ARIEL   That's my noble master!
  What shall I do? Say what? What shall I do?

PROSPERO   Go make thyself like a nymph o' th' sea. Be subject
  To no sight but thine and mine, invisible
  To every eyeball else. Go take this shape,   305
  And hither come in't. Go! Hence with diligence!°
                                    *Exit [*ARIEL]
  Awake, dear heart, awake! Thou hast slept well.
  Awake!

MIRANDA   The strangeness of your story put
  Heaviness in me.

PROSPERO   Shake it off. Come on;
  We'll visit Caliban, my slave, who never   310
  Yields us kind answer.

MIRANDA   'Tis a villain, sir,
  I do not love to look on.

PROSPERO   But as 'tis,
  We cannot miss° him. He does make our fire,
  Fetch in our wood, and serves in offices
  That profit us. What ho! Slave! Caliban,   315
  Thou earth, thou! Speak!

CALIBAN   *(Within)*   There's wood enough within.

PROSPERO   Come forth, I say! There's other business for thee.
  Come, thou tortoise! When?

Enter ARIEL *like a water nymph.*

  Fine apparition! My quaint° Ariel,
  Hark in thine ear.   *[Whispers.]*

ARIEL   My lord, it shall be done.   *Exit.* 320

echoing cries of "What shall I do?" (302) suggest limitless possibilities.

submissive*

duties as a sprite

303-06 No explanation is given for the disguise, but Ariel does not question; perhaps he laughs. In a moment, without a word, he is gone. As Prospero's order comes without hesitation—it can seem long-prepared or a sudden inspiration—so he insists on speedy action; again he is very aware of the need to effect everything within fixed time-limits.

307 All harshness vanishes in Prospero, as he bends over his daughter and speaks with gentle affection. But he remains in command: he may hold his staff over her to break the spell; there may be music.

speed, dispatch

309-16 Prospero's imperatives to rouse the sleepy Miranda and his insistence on visiting his other "slave" Caliban (l. 315; for the comparison with Ariel, see l. 272) are motivated only by his unspoken thoughts and decisions. The audience is surprised because an earlier mention of Caliban is all the preparation for this turn of events. The episode that follows supplies no explanation either, since making a "fire" (l. 313) has no direct effect on the action. The actor of Prospero, seeking a motive on which to base his performance, may conclude that the father wishes to confront his daughter with Caliban so that she will think the better of the man whom he wishes her to marry. But this supposes that Prospero is more anxious about the success of his own plans (and the good qualities of Ferdinand) than he is about the effect on Miranda of a reminder of Caliban's sexual assault (see ll. 349-50); perhaps that is appropriate, so innocent is Miranda despite her stated abhorrence of the "villain" (see ll. 312, 353, 361-62).

do without

Shakespeare accentuated the apparent arbitrariness of this transition by making Miranda reluctant to agree and Prospero sure that he will not receive "kind answer" (l. 311). Moreover it is hard to accept that they are unable to manage without Caliban's help (see l. 313) when Prospero can effect such complicated magic as the sea storm without it. (Another mystery is associated earlier with Caliban's mother; see lines 268-69.)

316-22 Caliban's rough, offstage cry contrasts with Ariel's first cry. Both audience and Prospero look in his direction and then, quite unexpectedly, Ariel has returned and is standing on the other side of the stage in the body of a nymph. Only Prospero's words identify him in his changed sexuality. His light, dart-

fine, clever

PROSPERO   Thou poisonous slave, got° by the devil himself
Upon thy wicked dam, come forth!

Enter CALIBAN.

CALIBAN   As wicked° dew as e'er my mother brushed
With raven's feather from unwholesome fen
Drop on you both. A southwest blow on ye,   325
And blister you all o'er.

PROSPERO   For this, be sure tonight thou shalt have cramps,
Side-stitches that shall pen thy breath up. Urchins°
Shall, for that vast° of night that they may work,
All exercise° on thee; thou shalt be pinched   330
As thick as honeycomb, each pinch more stinging
Than bees that made 'em.

CALIBAN   I must eat my dinner.
This island's mine by Sycorax my mother,
Which thou tak'st from me. When thou cam'st first,
Thou strok'st me and made much of me; wouldst give me   335
Water with berries in't; and teach me how
To name the bigger light, and how the less,°
That burn by day and night. And then I loved thee,
And showed thee all the qualities o' th' isle,
The fresh springs, brine pits, barren place and fertile—   340
Cursed be I that did so! All the charms
Of Sycorax, toads, beetles, bats, light° on you!
For I am all the subjects that you have,
Which first was mine own king; and here you sty° me
In this hard rock, whiles you do keep from me   345
The rest o' th' island.

PROSPERO   Thou most lying slave,
Whom stripes° may move, not kindness! I have used thee,
Filth as thou art, with humane care, and lodged thee
In mine own cell, till thou didst seek to violate
The honor of my child.   350

CALIBAN   O ho, O ho! Would't had been done!
Thou didst prevent me; I had peopled else
This isle with Calibans.

begotten

baneful

goblins

dead and empty time

perform their office*

(biblical; see *Genesis* i. 16:
"And God made...the
greater light to rule the day,
and the lesser light to rule
the night")

fall

pen up (as in a pigsty)*

lashes

ing movements and quiet obedience awaken a sense of imminent magic, made more mysterious by the whispered talk. For a moment Prospero is changed, delighting in his "quaint Ariel"; but he turns back with renewed imprecations to the "earth", the "tortoise", the "poisonous" and devilish Caliban (ll. 316, 318, 321).

323-46 A suitable entry for Caliban from his "rock" is through a trapdoor, especially so if Ariel has flown onto the stage from above—as he could have done with Jacobean stage machinery. Caliban's curse starts with refined precision. But by line 326, he has lost control and stops: the incomplete verse-line suggests that he falls silent; or he might relapse into the brutish "gabble" that was his by inheritance (see ll. 356-60). Miranda will draw back, accentuating Prospero's immediate confrontation of Caliban with threats of punishment. Caliban may cringe and suffer in anticipation—not unlike Ariel—but this "slave" is not cowed. He returns to the attack with the simplest assertion of his own rights to eat (l. 332) and to inherit the island from his mother; whereas Ariel had asked for "liberty" (l. 247), Caliban demands possession, and he reaches his demands the sooner. His rebellion is absolute; it is he, and not Prospero, who recalls the past in detail, reproaching the usurper for ingratitude and cruelty. Caliban's talk about gentle caresses, succor and education, and of love reciprocated and generous trust, establishes a new tone in the play; he makes a strong claim on the audience's sympathy, drawing it away from Prospero. Because Caliban is ugly and monstrous (see ll. 285-86), this tenderness is doubly effective.

346-53 Prospero is confident in his judgement: attempted rape has put Caliban beyond the pale of humanity. But Caliban's response is delighted; even while acknowledging failure, he asserts his virility and his ownership of the island. Presumably Miranda avoids looking at Caliban, who usually makes obscene gestures along with his laughter.

353-67 Many editors give this speech to Prospero, arguing that it is too severe for Miranda and implies too great a knowledge of the world; besides Caliban has said that Prospero taught him to speak (see ll. 336-38). But without it, Miranda would drop out of focus and the encounter that Prospero has insisted upon would not be fully enacted. If Miranda overcomes her aversion to turn and answer Caliban, she shows strength of mind as well as recalling on earlier, instinctive sympathy.

MIRANDA   Abhorrèd slave,
Which any print of goodness wilt not take,
Being capable of° all ill! I pitied thee,   355
Took pains to make thee speak, taught thee each hour
One thing or other. When thou didst not, savage,
Know thine own meaning, but wouldst gabble like
A thing most brutish, I endowed thy purposes
With words that made them known. But thy vile race,°   360
Though thou didst learn, had that in't which good natures
Could not abide to be with. Therefore wast thou
Deservedly confined into this rock, who hadst
Deserved more than a prison.

CALIBAN   You taught me language, and my profit on't   365
Is, I know how to curse. The red plague rid° you
For learning me your language!

PROSPERO   Hagseed,° hence!
Fetch us in fuel; and be quick, thou'rt best,°
To answer other business. Shrug'st thou, malice?
If thou neglect'st or dost unwillingly   370
What I command, I'll rack° thee with old° cramps,
Fill all thy bones with aches, make thee roar
That beasts shall tremble at thy din.

CALIBAN   No, pray thee.
   [Aside] I must obey. His art is of such power,
It would control° my dam's god, Setebos,   375
And make a vassal of him.

PROSPERO   So slave, hence!   *Exit* CALIBAN.

Enter FERDINAND; *and* ARIEL *[like a water nymph], invisible, playing and
singing.*

                                                                              380
ARIEL   *(Sings.)* Come unto these yellow sands,
                   And then take hands.
                Curtsied when you have and kissed
                   The wild waves whist,°
                Foot it featly° here and there;
                And, sweet sprites, the burden bear.°   385
                Hark, hark!

susceptible to

The half-line, 364, suggests that Caliban is momentarily silenced by Miranda (as he is not by Prospero); he replies at first reasonably, but then cries out for her death.

inherited disposition

367-76 Prospero intervenes as Caliban curses Miranda. Caliban usually continues to "gabble" (see l. 358), "shrugging" (see l. 369) and expressing resistance by any means except coherent speech. He finds his voice only to submit with a brevity which is unusual for him; but it is under compulsion as his following aside—the first in the play—makes obvious. His silent acquiescence to Prospero last order (l. 376) may carry a renewed threat in the manner in which he moves offstage. Alternatively, his aside can express total subservience and he may be too weak to resist dismissal; already he may be roaring, punished because submits "unwillingly" (l. 370). Although the episode with Caliban is much shorter than Prospero's duologues with Miranda and with Ariel, it starts at a high pitch and is strongly dramatic. It accomplishes little toward the progress of the play's action, but, while repeating questions of rights, betrayal, service and freedom, it demonstrates more completely the repressiveness and deliberate functioning of Prospero's power; it uncovers passions and tenderness, develops an impression of the natural resources of the island (to which Prospero appears unresponsive), brings a witch and the Devil into the story, and shows by Caliban's laughter and continued resistance, the limitations of Prospero's and Miranda's influence. It also encourages an audience to question Prospero's motives.

make away with, kill (wordplay on *red*)

hag's offspring
you'd better

torture   plenty of

overpower

377-89 "Sweet" music (l. 396) is a sudden contrast. Usually Ariel, in the guise of a nymph, enters first, dancing and playing on a pipe. His singing is gentle, sensuous, and courteous, like the words of his song; for the moment an audience is charmed into forgetting other dramatic issues. But the voices of a chorus of spirits, coming from all sides of the stage, evoke nighttime and danger, intimating the darker issues of the two previous episodes.

The "sprites", the "meaner ministers" of III.iii.87, may enter on the stage to sing the chorus, but the text does not require this; offstage voices can be sufficiently awesome and mysterious. On stage, the spirits would have to act, with Ariel, as if invisible to Ferdinand.

silent
dance neatly, nimbly
keep the refrain going

Prospero watches, wholly pleased: Ariel's embodiment as a seductive nymph—which makes his song the more alluring—was chosen to prepare Ferdinand for responding to Miranda. Prospero's

                     Burden (dispersedly)°: "Bow, wow!"
                     The watchdogs bark.
[*Burden (dispersedly)*]: "Bow, wow!"
                     Hark, hark! I hear
                     The strain of strutting chanticleer
                     Cry cock-a-diddle-dow.

FERDINAND Where should this music be? I' th' air or th' earth?   390
  It sounds no more; and sure it waits upon
  Some god o' th' island. Sitting on a bank,
  Weeping again° the king my father's wreck,
  This music crept by me upon the waters,
  Allaying both their fury and my passion°   395
  With its sweet air. Thence I have followed it,
  Or it hath drawn me rather; but 'tis gone.
  No, it begins again.

ARIEL   *(Sings.)* Full fathom five thy father lies,
                     Of his bones are coral made;   400
                     Those are pearls that were his eyes;
                     Nothing of him that doth fade,
                     But doth suffer a sea change
                     Into something rich and strange.
                     Sea nymphs hourly ring his knell: 405
                               Burden: "Ding-dong."
                     Hark! Now I hear them—ding-dong bell.

FERDINAND The ditty does remember my drowned father.
  This is no mortal business, nor no sound
  That the earth owes.° I hear it now above me.   410

PROSPERO The fringèd curtains of thine eye advance°
  And say what thou seest yond.

MIRANDA   What is't? A spirit?
  Lord, how it looks about!° Believe me sir,
  It carries° a brave form. But 'tis a spirit.

PROSPERO No, wench. It eats and sleeps, and hath such senses   415
  As we have, such. This gallant which thou seest
  Was in the wreck; and, but he's something stained°
  With grief, that's beauty's canker, thou mightst call him
  A goodly person. He hath lost his fellows,
  And strays about to find 'em.

from all parts (of the stage)

soul "prompts" the two young people (l. 423), but he knows that the success of the encounter depends on their affections given freely and their exchange of "eyes" (l. 444); he does all he can, therefore, to influence the meeting.

Miranda has probably been charmed into another sleep (perhaps still, magically, standing) and Prospero does not wake her until line 411. Certainly she does not see Ferdinand until then. And he is so entranced by the music that he does not see her.

responsively, over and over

passionate grief

390-98 As soon as Ariel has imitated the "strutting" bird of dawn (ll. 388-89), Ferdinand is roused and speaks. He looks in all directions, but then the music stops and he is still, sensing that he is in the presence of some unseen "god" (l. 392). He has been "weeping" (393), but now his long phrases (ll. 392-l. 96) suggest a rapt, reflective mood. As the spell weakens, he becomes more alert (see ll. 396-97), but when the music starts again he falls silent at once, listening.

399-410 The second song, in strong contrast, is about death not love, the dissolution of a human body and not courtly and delicate love-making. The music continues after the singing. Ariel may fly "above" Ferdinand (l. 410) to play the music on his pipe or the melody is reproduced above and around the stage by other means. Bells, or voices imitating them, may provide continuous and elaborate tolling. In any case, Ariel remains in view to Prospero and the audience, attentive for further orders. Ferdinand is brought close to tears (see ll. 437-38); he has also become more apprehensive (ll. 409-10)

owns

lift up

is on the watch

presents

disfigured

411-25 Prospero wakes Miranda, more delicate and formal in his speech than before; but at line 415 he is forthright, warm and humorous—although far less than open about what he has arranged for his daughter to witness.

The two young people are usually kept apart by Ariel, who sometimes plays on his pipe to do so, or directs movement rather like a policeman on traffic duty. He leads Ferdinand around the stage and charms him still. Just before "looks about" (l. 413) and "strays about" (l. 420), he may turn Ferdinand away from Miranda's approaches. At first she is wonder-struck (ll. 412-14) and her simplicity and eagerness may well cause the audience to laugh, and possibly Prospero. But then a stronger rhythm at lines 420-22 shows her feelings to be deep and sustaining—an impression accentuated by her father's lighter tone.

MIRANDA   I might call him   420
A thing divine, for nothing natural°
I ever saw so noble.

PROSPERO   *[Aside]*   It goes on, I see,
As my soul prompts it.—Spirit, fine spirit, I'll free thee
Within two days for this.

FERDINAND   Most sure the goddess
On whom these airs° attend! Vouchsafe° my prayer   425
May know if you remain° upon this island,
And that you will some good instruction give
How I may bear me° here. My prime request,
Which I do last pronounce,° is—O you wonder!—
If you be maid or no?

MIRANDA   No wonder,° sir,   430
But certainly a maid.

FERDINAND   My language? Heavens!
I am the best of them that speak this speech,
Were I but where 'tis spoken.

PROSPERO   How? The best?
What wert thou if the King of Naples heard thee?

FERDINAND   A single° thing, as I am now, that wonders   435
To hear thee speak of Naples. He does hear me;°
And that he does, I weep. Myself am Naples,
Who with mine eyes, never since at ebb, beheld
The king my father wrecked.

MIRANDA   Alack, for mercy!

FERDINAND   Yes, faith, and all his lords, the Duke of Milan   440
And his brave son° being twain.

PROSPERO   *[Aside]*   The Duke of Milan
And his more braver daughter could control° thee,
If now 'twere fit to do't. At the first sight
They have changed eyes.° Delicate° Ariel,
I'll set thee free for this. *[To* FERDINAND*]* A word good sir,   445
I fear you have done yourself some wrong.° A word!

MIRANDA   Why speaks my father so ungently? This

in nature

Now, with quickening rhythms, Prospero delights in the meeting, and also in Ariel, whose desire for freedom he now accepts instinctively.
At line 424, Ferdinand is released from his spell and sees Miranda. He too is wonder-struck, and kneels or retreats as if in the actual presence of a goddess. No spell is needed now to keep the two apart: Ariel stands back, at his master's side, his task done; he may laugh.

(Ariel's music)   deign to
grant
dwell

conduct myself

my petition of first importance
(*prime*) which I humbly
(*last*) declare

(wordplay on *Miranda* = wonder)

425-34   Miranda does not answer Ferdinand's "prayer" at once. When she does reply to his later "request"—it makes more sense to her—he recognizes, with a shock, that she is real, human, not at all alien, and unlikely to be above his own station in life: he is probably thinking about marriage already. Prospero steps forward to intervene (l. 433) and prevent too rapid developments. Miranda is left speechless and probably—in view of the assured tone of lines 430-31—awkwardly so.

poor/solitary/sincere

(Ferdinand thinks himself king now)

(the only mention on Antonio's son)

435-46   In his amazement, Ferdinand struggles to keep his dignity, even though he "weeps" in doing so (l. 437). Miranda responds quickly, but she probably does not approach him because he continues to speak only of his loss. Prospero speaks now jokingly, and probably aside: success is within view. He turns to Ariel and shares his pleasure, promising freedom—this time without mention of delay. As he does so Ferdinand and Miranda are free to approach each other until he intervenes again, this time "ungently" (l. 447).

refute, take to task

gazed at each other, fallen in
love   skillful, graceful

are mistaken (ironic)

447-52   Ferdinand turns to face his challenger, but is too confused to reply verbally. Nor does Miranda try to intervene, but speaks to herself (she is very used to being on her own), to "pity," or to any invisible power that might hear.
Now Ferdinand turns to gaze incredulously or uncomprehendingly towards Miranda; his next words

Is the third man that e'er I saw; the first
That e'er I sighed for. Pity move my father
To be inclined my way.

FERDINAND   O, if a virgin,   450
And your affection not gone forth, I'll make you
The Queen of Naples.

PROSPERO   Soft sir, one word more.
[Aside] They are both in either's powers. But this swift business
I must uneasy make, lest too light° winning
Make the prize light.° *[To* FERDINAND*]* One word more! I charge
    thee   455
That thou attend me. Thou dost here usurp
The name thou ow'st° not, and hast put thyself
Upon this island as a spy, to win it
From me, the lord on't.

FERDINAND   No, as I am a man.

MIRANDA   There's nothing ill can dwell in such a temple.   460
If the ill spirit have so fair a house,
Good things will strive to dwell with't.

PROSPERO   Follow me.
[To MIRANDA*]* Speak not you for him; he's a traitor.—Come,
I'll manacle thy neck and feet together.
Sea water shalt thou drink; thy food shall be   465
The fresh-brook mussels, withered roots, and husks
Wherein the acorn cradled. Follow!

FERDINAND   No.
I will resist such entertainment,° till
Mine enemy has more power.

                    He draws, and is charmed from moving.

MIRANDA   O dear father,
Make not too rash a trial of him, for   470
He's gentle° and not fearful.°

PROSPERO   What, I say,
My foot my tutor?°—Put thy sword up, traitor,
Who mak'st a show, but dar'st not strike, thy conscience
Is so possessed with guilt. Come from thy ward,°

are addressed to her. He is ready by this time, to offer, with full consciousness of royal responsibilities, the devotion of his whole life to this hitherto unknown person.

452-59   A third time Prospero intervenes, but Ferdinand again does not reply. A spell probably stops response while he continues to speak aside. Ariel may help in this by drawing (see l. 397) Ferdinand and Miranda apart from the other.

easy
little valued

ownest

Hiding his own pleasure, Prospero returns to Ferdinand and lays very severe charges against him. An audience is well aware that he is acting a role for his own ends, but Prospero seems harsh and too apprehensive about the strong feelings he has aroused in the young man. Much depends on the actor's interpretation of Prospero and to what extent Ariel's assistance has given rise to light-hearted fun.

Ferdinand denies the charges strenuously and may be perplexed still more as Ariel plays some trick which makes him appear childish and no "man" (l. 459).

460-69   It is Miranda who intervenes now. Presumably she is repeating a lesson she has been taught by her father, for she cannot speak from experience. Prospero reacts by becoming still more severe to Ferdinand. With no apparent respect for her feelings or for the truth, he pauses briefly to silence Miranda and then threatens and seeks to repress Ferdinand in the same manner as he has previously dealt with Ariel and Caliban (see ll. 287-98, 327-32).

Ferdinand's defiant "No" suggests sudden and quick action, which is then made ridiculous by a spell that keeps him frozen in an aggressive attitude. Ariel, invisible to Ferdinand, is often instrumental in this arrest.

treatment

Prospero's repeated praise for Ariel makes best sense if the spirit has taken part in all the trickery of this scene; this has the additional advantage of making the operation of the magic more obvious and at the same time leaving Prospero free to maintain a totally severe front to Ferdinand and Miranda.

469-89   Fearful for Ferdinand, Miranda runs to her father. By line 477, she is clinging to him, desperate because of his apparent blindness and cruelty. As Prospero reproves her and demonstrates his complete domination of Ferdinand, she offers herself as his "surety" (l. 478).

of noble birth, courteous
frightening
does a small part of me, my
daughter, presume to
instruct me
drop your guard

At line 476, Ferdinand's sword which he can no longer move drops from his hand, rendering him

For I can here disarm thee with this stick,°   475
And make thy weapon drop.

MIRANDA   Beseech you, father.

PROSPERO   Hence! Hang not on my garments.

MIRANDA   Sir, have pity.
I'll be his surety.

PROSPERO   Silence! One word more
Shall make me chide thee, if not hate thee. What,
An advocate for an impostor? Hush!   480
Thou think'st there is no more such shapes as he
Having seen but him and Caliban. Foolish wench,
To th' most of men this is a Caliban,
And they to him are angels.

MIRANDA   My affections
Are then most humble; I have no ambition   485
To see a goodlier man.

PROSPERO   [To FERDINAND] Come on, obey!
Thy nerves° are in their infancy again
And have no vigor in them.

FERDINAND   So they are.
My spirits, as in a dream, are all bound up.
My father's loss, the weakness which I feel,   490
The wreck of all my friends, nor this man's threats
To whom I am subdued,° are but light° to me,
Might I but through my prison once a day
Behold this maid. All corners else o' th' earth
Let liberty° make use of: space enough   495
Have I in such a prison.

PROSPERO   [Aside]   It works. [To FERDINAND] Come on.
[To ARIEL] Thou hast done well, fine° Ariel! [To FERDINAND]
    Follow me.
[To ARIEL] Hark what thou else shalt do me.

MIRANDA   Be of comfort.
My father's of a better nature, sir,
Than he appears by speech. This is unwonted   500
Which now came from him.

i.e., Prospero's magic staff
(ironically belittling)

even more ridiculous; he may struggle, uselessly, to voice a protest (see ll. 478-80).

As Prospero reminds Miranda of Caliban, whom he has just shown to her (see commentary, ll. 309-16), he lies preposterously. An audience, which has also just seen the "freckled whelp...not honored with a human shape" (ll. 285-6), will appreciate how deceitful and repressive Prospero is prepared to be (or, at best, how much he overplays his hand) in order to restrain the lovers.

Miranda is quietened but not diverted; her next words (ll. 484-86) are steadier and more determined.

Prospero now turns back to Ferdinand, releasing him from his spell-imposed trance, but still limiting his freedom (see ll. 487-88); he stumbles, falls and speaks weakly.

sinews

489-97 Ferdinand struggles to understand, but accepts that he is being taken off to "prison" (l. 493). From the first, however, he is sure about the vision he has seen and his devotion to Miranda is unshakeable: the syntax shows that his affirmation of this starts with line 490.

As soon as Ferdinand refers to "this maid" (l. 494), he realizes that in his mind he is still free; in contrast to Ariel and Caliban when they were faced with Prospero's threats and manifestations of superhuman power, Ferdinand dares to say that he is almost unconquerable.

made subject   easily borne

Ferdinand's strong, up-beat ending leads Prospero to respond with strong and simple phrases (l. 496), as if he has caught something of his enthusiasm. However these words can be spoken with a contrary and deflating asperity and coldness, real or pretended. Only when Prospero takes time to turn to Ariel does his sense of satisfaction become explicit; he may share some sense of mischief with his spirit.

those who are free

accomplished

498-504 While Prospero continues to instruct Ariel inaudibly, Miranda crosses to Ferdinand to comfort him. She usually kneels at his side as he lies, weakened, on the ground. Since Ferdinand makes no reply, they may again be briefly "spell-stopped" (see V.i.61).

When Prospero has promised Ariel freedom, he re-exerts his power over the two lovers with brisk

PROSPERO   Thou shalt be as free
   As mountain winds; but then° exactly° do
   All points° of my command.

ARIEL   To th' syllable.

PROSPERO*[To* FERDINAND*]* Come, follow. *[To* MIRANDA*]*
   Speak not for him.   *Exeunt.*

in that case   perfectly

details

commands, separating them and silencing Miranda. The small procession off stage will almost certainly be comically clumsy: Ferdinand struggles to hide his weakness, Miranda to obey her father. Prospero has forced the scene to a close.

Sometimes Ariel remains onstage until the others have gone; only when he has silently conducted the king and courtiers into view for Act II does he fly off.

ACT II

Scene i   *Enter* ALONSO, SEBASTIAN, ANTONIO, GONZALO, ADRIAN,
FRANCISCO, *and others.*

GONZALO   Beseech you sir, be merry. You have cause—
So have we all—of joy; for our escape
Is much beyond our loss. Our hint° of woe
Is common; every day some sailor's wife,
The masters of some merchant,° and the merchant,   5
Have just our theme of woe. But for the miracle—
I mean our preservation—few in millions
Can speak like us. Then wisely, good sir, weigh
Our sorrow with our comfort.

ALONSO   Prithee peace.

SEBASTIAN   *[Aside]* He receives comfort like cold porridge.°   10

ANTONIO   *[Aside]* The visitor° will not give him o'er° so.

SEBASTIAN   *[Aside]* Look, he's winding up the watch of his wit;
by and by it will strike.

GONZALO   Sir.

SEBASTIAN   *[Aside]* One.° Tell.°   15

GONZALO   When every grief is entertained that's offered,
Comes to th' entertainer—

SEBASTIAN   A dollar.°

GONZALO   Dolor comes to him, indeed: you have spoken truer
than you purposed.   20

SEBASTIAN   You have taken it wiselier than I meant you should.

GONZALO   Therefore, my lord . . .

ANTONIO   Fie, what a spendthrift is he of his tongue!

ALONSO   I prithee, spare.°

GONZALO   Well, I have done. But yet . . .   25

SEBASTIAN   He will be talking.

occasion

owners of some merchant ship

soup containing peas (pun on
peace)
parish visitor of the sick and
needy   release him / pronounce him incurable

he has struck one   keep count

in payment for *entertain*ment)

forbear

1-9 The short rhythms, varying syntax and the fact
that he does not mention the loss of Ferdinand which
most concerns the king he is trying to comfort (see ll.
104, 106-08), all suggest that Gonzalo's first speech
has a nervous energy and hides his own anxiety.
With "miracle" (l. 6) he thinks he has gone too far and
takes time to explain, carefully watching to see how
Alonso takes what he says.

The beginning of this scene lacks clear development and is often heavily cut for performance.
Nervous expectation and frustration are both essential; each ploy of the courtiers should be played
strongly and precisely, before it fails in its purpose
and a fully-charged silence follows. Although he says
little, Alonso takes the center stage and is referred to
with all possible respect; so the talk will ricochet
around him, often showing its force in the laughter of
others or in the wounds the king silently bears.

Alonso's brief reply (l. 9) can be curt, firm or
weary; he probably turns away from his courtiers, or
sits with his head buried in his hands. For a moment
all will be quiet, but the courtiers' unaccustomed
insecurity can be communicated to an audience
through their physical uneasiness.

10-26 By talking aside and laughing, Sebastian and
Antonio show a lack of sympathy and restless minds
which do not defer to a king. Gonzalo's determination
to continue his attempt to comfort the king appears to
be both funnier and more persistent by contrast with
their pursuit of cheap jokes. At first the old councilor
seems not to hear or not to heed their mockery, but
at line 19 he turns on them briefly, answering them in
their own coin. He turns back to the king only to hes-
itate (l. 22): Alonso has probably looked up at
Gonzalo and silenced him by obvious signs of grief
on his face.

The entire party had entered in search of
Ferdinand (see l. 316: "further search"), but no one
has dared to mention this. Gonzalo does not know
how to proceed and is mocked for that by Antonio.
Alonso says only "I prithee, spare" (l. 24) and
Gonzalo accepts the reproof, only to begin once
more and then withdraw before saying anything to
his purpose. Sebastian caps this by supplying words
that seem irrefutable (l. 26); he and Antonio probably
laugh together.

ANTONIO   Which, of he or Adrian, for a good wager, first begins to
    crow?

SEBASTIAN   The old cock.°

ANTONIO   The cock'rel.   30

SEBASTIAN   Done! The wager?°

ANTONIO   A laughter.°

SEBASTIAN   A match!°

ADRIAN   Though this island seem to be desert—

ANTONIO   Ha, ha, ha!   35

SEBASTIAN   So, you're paid.

ADRIAN   Uninhabitable, and almost inaccessible—

SEBASTIAN   Yet—

ADRIAN   Yet—

ANTONIO   He could not miss't.   40

ADRIAN   It must needs be of subtle,° tender, and delicate° temper-
    ance.°

ANTONIO   Temperance° was a delicate° wench.

SEBASTIAN   Ay, and a subtle,° as he most learnedly delivered.

ADRIAN   The air breathes upon us here most sweetly.   45

SEBASTIAN   As if it had lungs, and rotten ones.

ANTONIO   Or as 'twere perfumed by a fen.°

GONZALO   Here is everything advantageous to life.

ANTONIO   True; save means to live.

SEBASTIAN   Of that there's none, or little.   50

GONZALO   How lush and lusty the grass looks! How green!

ANTONIO   The ground indeed is tawny.

SEBASTIAN   With an eye° of green in't.

ANTONIO   He misses not much.°

i.e., Gonzalo

27-28 Antonio may walk further away from the king, followed by Sebastian. They sit down and survey the bewildered survivors critically. They seem the most self-possessed and assured.

stake, prize

he who wins will laugh (pun on *laughter* = a clutch of eggs)

agreed

29-47 Adrian and Gonzalo both walk up and down, like cock-birds in a pen. Adrian does not keep the lords waiting to see who wins the wager, but begins at once, with a subsidiary clause of the speech he has been preparing. He is more formal, less personal, than Gonzalo. Although he does not address Alonso, he is very conscious of being in the royal presence and his eye will keep coming back to the king. He pauses to choose appropriate words and form, to the amusement of the mocking onlookers; probably he does not even hear that they are speaking.

At lines 43-44, the commentators, in apparent seriousness, agree with Adrian, as if he had been talking of quite other matters.

Lines 46-47 could be addressed directly to a bemused Adrian; alternatively, at line 45 he runs out of comments to make: either way, he retreats from his attempt to foster optimism.

fine   delightful   climate

(Puritan first name)   pampered

sly, crafty

march, bog

48-55 Gonzalo takes over, supporting what Adrian has been saying; then he, too, pauses. Relentlessly, the comment continues *sotto voce*; lines 52-53 introduce a new discriminating tone which may indicate that they are offered directly to Gonzalo, who considers the opinion carefully before proceeding. Sebastian's deflating comment at line 55 rings true in that Gonzalo has indeed mistaken the "truth" of Alonso's grief for his son; what the island is like is immaterial to him. Indeed Gonzalo's references to "life" and the "lush and lusty" grass might well accentuate the king's grief, if he has been listening, by awakening memories of spring-time and youth.

tinge

Alonso remains the silent—probably unmoving—center of attention.

(ironic)

SEBASTIAN   No. He doth but mistake the truth totally.   55

GONZALO   But the rarity° of it is—which is indeed almost beyond
    credit—

SEBASTIAN   As many vouched rarities are.

GONZALO   That our garments, being, as they were, drenched in
    the sea, hold, notwithstanding, their freshness and glosses,   60
    being rather new-dyed than stained with salt water.

ANTONIO   If but one of his pockets could speak, would it not say
    he lies?

SEBASTIAN   Ay, or very falsely pocket up° his report.

GONZALO   Methinks our garments are now as fresh as when we   65
    put them on first in Afric, at the marriage of the king's fair
    daughter Claribel to the King of Tunis.

SEBASTIAN   'Twas a sweet marriage, and we prosper well in our
    return.°

ADRIAN   Tunis was never graced before with such a paragon   70
    to° their queen.

GONZALO   Not since widow Dido's° time.

ANTONIO   Widow? A pox o' that! How came that "widow" in?
    Widow Dido!

SEBASTIAN   What if he had said "widower Aeneas" too? Good   75
    Lord, how you take it!

ADRIAN   "Widow Dido," said you? You make me study of that.
    She was of Carthage,° not of Tunis.

GONZALO   This Tunis, sir, was Carthage.

ADRIAN   Carthage?   80

GONZALO   I assure you, Carthage.

ANTONIO   His word is more than the miraculous harp.°

SEBASTIAN   He hath raised the wall, and houses too.

ANTONIO   What impossible matter will he make easy next?

SEBASTIAN   I think he will carry this island home in his pocket,   85
    and give it his son for an apple.

wonder

conceal

(ironic)

for

widow of King Sychaeus: mistress of Aeneas before Jupiter ordered his departure (Antonio mocks Gonzalo for avoiding an allusion to her more famous affair)

(destroyed in Punic wars)

(Ovid, the poet, wrote that Amphion raised the walls of Thebes by playing on his *harp*)

56-61 Gonzalo now mentions what may have been noticed by the audience from the beginning of the scene; his delayed awareness alerts attention for other clues to the meaning of this apparently idle episode.

With a more sustained speech, Gonzalo seems wholly caught up in the strangeness of events; he may forget, for the moment, to address Alonso. But the rhythms of what he says are broken and uneasy, expressing an underlying incredulity or fear.

62-64 Antonio may imply that Alonso (or, perhaps, Gonzalo himself) has been weeping "salt" tears, and Sebastian that Gonzalo is only acting his cheerfulness: if so, these critics, who are said to "laugh at nothing" (ll. 168-69), are the first to force others to acknowledge what has lain behind the words they speak.

65-72 Gonzalo so far forgets decorum that, after a brief silence, he speaks about the king in his presence (his phrases lengthening as his confidence grows) and again disobeys the royal command for "peace" (9). Sebastian quickly underlines Gonzalo's *gaffe* with sharp irony (l. 68) that will cut deeply: Alonso, reminded of the loss of his daughter as well as his son (see l. 104), may cry out in grief.

Adrian intervenes to brighten the talk (l. 70), and Gonzalo seconds his effort with a pedantic and discreetly expressed caveat that causes a diversion, and was probably intended to do so (see ll. 166-69).

73-88 Adrian questions slowly, and Gonzalo's confident reply does not unconvince him (l. 80). However, Antonio and Sebastian have been deflected from talking about the king's loss and revert to quick and shallow amusement at Gonzalo's expense. After line 81, Gonzalo turns back to the king and considers silently how best to counter his grief with lighter talk—which doctors of the time prescribed as a cure for melancholy.

The badinage concludes with a bizarre fantasy on the themes of possession and fecundity. By playing the fool, the two lords have come closest to the truth about the island; their words have odd and unwitting echoes of earlier episodes involving Ferdinand and Caliban.

ANTONIO   And sowing the kernels of it in the sea, bring forth
    more islands.

GONZALO   I—

ANTONIO   Why, in good time.   90

GONZALO   [*To* ALONSO] Sir, we were talking that our garments
    seem now as fresh as when we were at Tunis at the marriage
    of your daughter, who is now queen.

ANTONIO   And the rarest that e'er came there.

SEBASTIAN   Bate,° I beseech you, widow Dido.   95

ANTONIO   O, widow Dido! Ay, widow Dido.

GONZALO   Is not, sir, my doublet as fresh as the first day I wore
    it? I mean, in a sort.°

ANTONIO   That "sort" was well fished for.°

GONZALO   When I wore it at your daughter's marriage.   100

ALONSO   You cram° these words into mine ears against
    The stomach° of my sense. Would I had never
    Married my daughter there! For, coming thence,
    My son is lost; and, in my rate,° she too,
    Who is so far from Italy removed   105
    I ne'er again shall see her. O thou mine heir
    Of Naples and of Milan, what strange fish
    Hath made his meal on thee?

FRANCISCO   Sir, he may live.
    I saw him beat the surges under him,
    And ride upon their backs. He trod the water,   110
    Whose enmity he flung aside, and breasted
    The surge most swol'n that met him. His bold head
    'Bove the contentious waves he kept, and oared
    Himself with his good arms in lusty stroke
    To th' shore, that o'er his° wave-worn basis bowed,   115
    As stooping to relieve° him. I not doubt
    He came alive to land.

ALONSO   No, no, he's gone.

SEBASTIAN   Sir, you may thank yourself for this great loss,

don't count

to some extent/in a fashion

took some time to find/was
rescued after a long time in
water

force

inclination (pun on *cram* =
overfeed)

estimation

89-108   Closely watched by his sneering critics,
Gonzalo at last addresses the king. After a false start
he corrects himself, now using "we" (l. 91) and so
drawing the whole company into the conversation.
But phrasing and rhythms show that he soon loses
confidence. He reverts to speaking entirely about
himself (ll. 97-98) and then speaks of the wedding of
Alonso's daughter without ceremony and without
regard for the king's particular griefs (l. 100).
Gonzalo's own anxieties as a survivor in strange circumstances have drawn him to say the opposite of
what might be consoling.

Alonso, outs him off with his first sustained
speech in the play: as the dialogue moves back to
verse, he dominates the scene. His first images of
physical effort and revulsion are strong and commanding, but self-criticism and grief are expressed
with affecting simplicity, and perhaps with tears. His
last sentence suggests that he loses himself in bitter
and nightmarish fantasy, again cutting himself off
from his courtiers (ll. 107-08).

Francisco's opening sentence (l. 108) can be
spoken urgently and firmly, as he is the first to counsel hope; he prevents intervention by proceeding
with his tale at once.

its (the shore's)

succor/lift up

108-17   Active verbs give Francisco's careful and
elaborate speech an energy which supports his
hopeful message. Moreover this is an occasion when
Shakespeare has given a major task in the development of the scene to an actor with a very small role:
his concern to speak well and the sound of an entirely new voice will both attract attention, from the theatre audience as much as the one on stage. He concludes by repeating his first message (l. 108) with
much greater confidence, no longer "he may" live,
but "I not doubt" (ll. 115-16).

The rousing effect is broken by the king's sim-
ply-spoken despair (l. 117). Alonso may weep, or
walk away, retreating into his own thoughts once
more.

That would not bless our Europe with your daughter,
But rather loose° her to an African,   120
Where she, at least,° is banished from your eye,
Who hath cause to wet° the grief on't.°

ALONSO   Prithee peace.

SEBASTIAN   You were kneeled to, and importuned otherwise
By all of us; and the fair soul herself
Weighed° between loathness and obedience, at   125
Which end o' th' beam° should bow. We have lost your son,
I fear for ever. Milan and Naples have
Moe° widows in them of this business' making
Than we bring men to comfort them.
The fault's your own.

ALONSO   So is the dear'st° o' th' loss.   130

GONZALO   My lord Sebastian,
The truth you speak doth lack some gentleness,
And time° to speak in it. You rub the sore
When you should bring the plaster.

SEBASTIAN   Very well.

ANTONIO   And most chirurgeonly.°   135

GONZALO   [*To* ALONSO] It is foul weather in us all, good sir,
When you are cloudy.

SEBASTIAN   [*Aside*]   Foul weather?

ANTONIO   [*Aside*]   Very foul.°

GONZALO   Had I plantation° of this isle, my lord—

ANTONIO   [*Aside*] He'd sow't with nettle seed.°

SEBASTIAN   [*Aside*]   Or docks, or mallows.

GONZALO   And were the king on't, what would I do?   140

SEBASTIAN   [*Aside*] 'Scape being drunk, for want of wine.

GONZALO   I' th' commonwealth I would by contraries°
Execute all things. For no kind of traffic°
Would I admit; no name° of magistrate;
Letters° should not be known; riches, poverty,   145

(pun on *loss*, line 118)

to put it mildly

you have good cause to weep
on that account

balanced evenly

(of a scale)

more in number

most deeply felt

proper occasion

befitting a surgeon

(puns on *foul* = unfavorable,
wet filthy, rough, against
rules)

colonization

(pun on *plantation* = planting,
sowing)

contrary to usual practice/by
prohibitions

business

title

learning

118-30 Sebastian turns on his king and elder brother in outspoken criticism. He cuts through normal respect and flattery, and ignores a request for silence (l. 122). He deals more personally with the issues and consequences of the king's decisions—which he accounts for as he might the aftermath of defeat in battle (compare *Coriolanus*, *King John*, *Henry V*, etc.). Politically this is either surprisingly bold or unexpectedly foolish; it may be motivated by suppressed personal antagonism.

Having heard him out, Alonso speaks bitterly of his grief and then is silent (l. 130): his word are at the emotional center of the scene (until l. 301 arouses a new kind of fear and desperation). Played strongly, in contrast to all the oblique talk and ineffectual good intentions, this moment is most affecting, revealing a bankrupt but still suffering spirit. Line 131 is an incomplete verse-line, probably indicating a shocked pause following Alonso's admission.

131-38 Gonzalo reproaches Sebastian, but also acknowledges that he is his "lord" and that he has spoken the "truth" (l. 132) when others were avoiding it. The half-line shows that he waits for silence before trying to apologize for everyone to the king (ll. 136-37). With some hesitation, he starts a new topic for conversation to keep the peace and take the king's thoughts off his grief. The mocking commentary starts up again, but he ignores it.

142-63 This passage is based on John Florio's translation of Montaigne's *Essay*, "Of the Cannibals" (see Introduction). The piled-up description and emphatic negatives suggest a thoughtful energy of mind, or a very zealous recital of ready-made opinion.

Sebastian cuts in (l. 151) to point out a contradiction (another, lighter, telling of the "truth"; see previous note), but neither this nor laughter can silence Gonzalo now, or moderate his enthusiasm. Rather, he rises to a more general evocation of a Golden Age of fruitfulness and moral purity, such as poets imagined to have existed in an innocent past. Poets contemporary with Shakespeare shared this vision and they also imagined that the New World across the Atlantic offered opportunity to rediscover such a paradise; so Michael Drayton (ll. 1563-1631) praised Virginia, "Earth's only Paradise":

> Where Nature hath in store
> Foul, venison, and fish,
>   And the fruitful'st soil
>   Without your toil,

And use of service,° none; contract, succession,°
Bourn,° bound° of land, tilth,° vineyard, none;
No use of metal, corn, or wine, or oil;
No occupation; all men idle, all;
And women too, but innocent and pure;   150
No sovereignty—

SEBASTIAN   [Aside]   Yet he would be king on't.

ANTONIO   [Aside] The latter end of his commonwealth forgets the
    beginning.

GONZALO   All things in common nature should produce
    Without sweat or endeavor. Treason, felony,   155
    Sword, pike, knife, gun, or need of any engine°
    Would I not have; but nature should bring forth,
    Of it own kind,° all foison,° all abundance,
    To feed my innocent people.

SEBASTIAN   [Aside] No marrying 'mong his subjects?   160

ANTONIO   [Aside] None, man, all idle—whores and knaves.

GONZALO   I would with such perfection govern, sir,
    T' excel the Golden Age.°

SEBASTIAN   'Save His Majesty!

ANTONIO   Long live Gonzalo!

GONZALO   And—do you mark me, sir?

ALONSO   Prithee no more: thou dost talk nothing to me.   165

GONZALO   I do well believe Your Highness; and did it to min-
    ister occasion° to these gentlemen, who are of such sensi-
    ble° and nimble lungs that they always use to laugh° at
    nothing.

ANTONIO   'Twas you we laughed at.   170

GONZALO   Who, in this kind of merry fooling, am nothing to
    you; so you may continue, and laugh at nothing still.

ANTONIO   What a blow was there given!

SEBASTIAN   An° it had not fallen flatlong.°

serving a master   inheritance
boundary   enclosure   agriculture

Three harvests more,
All greater than your wish. . .

To whom the Golden Age
Still Nature's laws doth give,
No other cares attend,
But them to defend
From winter's rage,
That long there doth not live.

By the close of his account of plantation, Gonzalo
holds the stage, usurping attention from Alonso; he
may have forgotten whom he is addressing and be
lost in his own fantasy. He does not refer to the king
after line 138, until he hears the two lords claim that
he is recommending freedom for "whores and
knaves" (ll. 160-61).

weapon

An actor can make Gonzalo an enthusiastic revolutionary (although this does not agree with his def-
according to its own nature
plenty

erence elsewhere to authority), an idle talker, or a
fervent sentimentalist who enjoys day-dreaming
about peace. Such a "Golden Age" is neither jest,
dream, nor consolation, for Alonso (see l. 165); and
having seen Prospero's kingdom, with its subject
daughter, spirit and bestial insurgent, an audience
may make further critical comparisons.

Gonzalo's sustained speech also marks, by
contrast, the dispersed and nervous quality of the
mythical time of primitive per-
fection

rest of the dialogue, his own included. Then it yields
to renewed exchange of cheap sarcasm and recrim-
ination.

163-82   At lines 163-64, Sebastian and Antonio triv-
ialize the evocation of perfection with ironic bows and
laughter (see l. 168). When Gonzalo applies directly
to the king (l. 164), he is rebuffed, but bitterness and
tension have gone from Alonso's words. Gonzalo is
now free to turn on his tormentors, one of whom is
his lord and the other brother to the king. He tries to
give opportunity

sensitive   are in the habit of
laughing

disengage himself (ll. 171-72), then to send them up
with compliment (l. 175) and then to attack more
openly (ll. 175-77). His anger is about to overflow, but
is weakened by self-righteousness (ll. 179-81).

if   with the flat of the
sword/stupidly

GONZALO   You are a gentleman of brave mettle; you would lift 175
the moon out of her sphere, if she would continue in it five
weeks without changing.°

Enter ARIEL *[invisible] playing solemn music.*

SEBASTIAN   We would so, and then go a-batfowling.°

ANTONIO   Nay, good my lord, be not angry.

GONZALO   No, I warrant you; I will not adventure my discretion 180
so weakly.° Will you laugh me asleep, for I am very heavy?°

ANTONIO   Go sleep, and hear us.°
[All sleep except ALONSO, SEBASTIAN *and* ANTONIO.*]*
ALONSO   What, all so soon asleep? I wish mine eyes
Would, with themselves,° shut up my thoughts. I find
They are inclined to do so.

SEBASTIAN   Please you sir,   185
Do not omit° the heavy offer of it.
It° seldom visits sorrow; when it doth,
It is a comforter.

ANTONIO   We two, my lord,
Will guard your person while you take your rest,
And watch your safety.

ALONSO   Thank you.—Wondrous heavy.   190
                         *[*ALONSO *sleeps. Exit* ARIEL.*]*
SEBASTIAN   What a strange drowsiness possesses them!

ANTONIO   It is the quality o' th' climate. *Sleep magic*

SEBASTIAN   Why
Doth it not then our eyelids sink? I find not
Myself disposed to sleep.

ANTONIO   Nor I: my spirits are nimble.
They fell together all, as by consent;°   195
They dropped as by a thunderstroke. What might,
Worthy Sebastian? O, what might!—No more.—
And yet methinks I see it in thy face,
What thou shouldst be. Th' occasion speaks° thee, and

i.e., offer to do impossibilities,
under impossible conditions

catching birds (with the moon
for a lantern)/tricking fools

risk losing my good judgment
over so slight a matter
sleepy/sad

(laughing) .

as their lids close

neglect
sleep

agreement

calls to action/testifies to

Already Ariel has entered with music and in very short time all but three of those onstage have fallen asleep, quickly, unceremoniously and (from the audience's point of view, and Ariel's) comically. Ariel may move from one to another and cast his spell by touching each in turn; or, taking lines 195-96 literally, an abrupt climax in his music works on all together. Gonzalo speaks his last words struggling against sleep; Antonio taunts him with his promise that they will haunt his dreams.

183-90 While Alonso is speaking, Ariel casts his spell on his last victim, who says he is not sleepy but becomes drowsy and soon drops off to sleep. As this is happening Sebastian and Antonio are respectful and solicitous (ll. 185-90): they have not spoken so before, and their new style of address may be a reaction to the "solemn" music, or else an encouragement of their lord's weakness so that they may enjoy a more powerful position.

Once the king is asleep, only two are on their feet; they look around at their fellows stretched out in whatever place they "fell" (l. 195). Their first reaction may be amazement, their second laughter, and their third a mutual silence. Perhaps someone snores (see l. 293, below) or moves in his sleep. Perhaps Ariel has a final check that all is according to plan: the music stops; he may laugh or play a last unnecessary trick.

191-201 Antonio's first words after Alonso falls asleep are enigmatic or even careless in comparison with Sebastian's which could express a serious, responsible alarm. But Antonio's mind may be very active elsewhere, in his own "imagination" (l. 200). With only the briefest hesitation (l. 197)—and this may be a pretense—Antonio plays for the largest stakes. Yet he remains wary, making sure that Sebastian is ready to see things his way before he comes to the detail of his plan.

Probably Antonio does not move at first, only his eyes and sense of humor betraying his "nimble" spirits and "strong imagination." Sebastian on the other hand may go around looking at each of the sleepers. At line 196 or 197, Antonio goes to Sebastian, speaking quietly now.

My strong imagination sees a crown　　　　　　200
Dropping upon thy head.

SEBASTIAN　　　　　　　　What! Art thou waking?

ANTONIO　Do you not hear me speak?

SEBASTIAN　　　　　　　　　　I do; and surely
It is a sleepy language, and thou speak'st
Out of thy sleep. What is it thou didst say?
This is a strange repose, to be asleep　　　　205
With eyes wide open: standing, speaking, moving,
And yet so fast asleep.

ANTONIO　　　　　　　Noble Sebastian,
Thou let'st thy fortune sleep—die, rather—wink'st°
Whiles thou art waking.

SEBASTIAN　　　　　　Thou dost snore distinctly;
There's meaning in thy snores.　　　　　　210

ANTONIO　I am more serious than my custom. You
Must be so too, if heed me; which to do
Trebles thee o'er.°

SEBASTIAN　　　　　　Well, I am standing water.

ANTONIO　I'll teach you how to flow.

SEBASTIAN　　　　　　　　Do so: to ebb
Hereditary sloth° instructs me.

ANTONIO　　　　　　　　O,　　　　　215
If you but knew how you the purpose° cherish
Whiles thus you mock it; how, in stripping it,
You more invest° it! Ebbing men, indeed,
Most often do so near the bottom run°
By their own fear or sloth.

SEBASTIAN　　　　　　Prithee say on.　　　220
The setting° of thine eye and cheek proclaim
A matter° from thee; and a birth, indeed,
Which throes° thee much to yield.

ANTONIO　　　　　　　　Thus, sir:
Although this lord of weak remembrance,° this

hast thine eyes closed

202-15 Sebastian still appears to be involved with the "strange" events, but his attention has been caught; he may speak in order to cover his awakened ambition and his own imagination. When he speaks of "a strange repose" (l. 205) he is almost certainly referring to Antonio's suggestion which he had referred to cautiously, a moment before, as a "sleepy language" (l. 203). At line 206, he means that Antonio is "moving." him to action or that Antonio is going from one place to another making doubly sure that no one is listening. Either way it is clear that both are entering a highly dangerous situation.

Antonio now calls Sebastian "noble" to remind him of his royal blood; his jest on "die" (given edge by the possibility of murder) draws Sebastian on. But he still says as little as possible and watches closely, making a joke about "snores" (l. 210) which could be construed as evasion or encouragement. The vein of humor now is sharper and more economical than the earlier taunting of Gonzalo; very soon it becomes hard and head-on.

increases your fortunes three-fold

The short line 210 indicates that Antonio pauses before acknowledging that his purpose is "serious." By line 213, Sebastian is fully alert but, like Antonio, continues to play a waiting game, disguising it as self-deprecation and aristocratic laziness.

inherited laziness/being born a younger son

proposal

clothe/give (royal) power to

i.e., their fortunes touch rock bottom

215-23 Antonio's "O" may indicate some impatience before telling Sebastian that he knows his words have had a double purpose and that he will pretend that he does not know that Sebastian knows. He then plays upon his hearer's pride by attacking him for "fear or sloth" (l. 220).

Sebastian ignores all this, being quite able to recognize the immediate issues. He forces Antonio to take full initiative (l. 220). His reading of Antonio's face (ll. 221-22) announces that he is watching very closely and that nothing will escape attention.

fixed expression

theme of importance

pains (pun on *matter* = pus)

With "Thus, sir" (l. 223), Antonio may conduct Sebastian further from the sleeping king or sit down beside him.

failing memory

224-38 Antonio talks in a less challenging, more conversational manner; quiet, still and relaxed, he is ready now to unfold his plot. But his syntax is com-

Who shall be of as little memory°   225
When he is earthed,° hath here almost persuaded—
For he's a spirit of persuasion; only
Professes to persuade°—the king his son's alive,
'Tis as impossible that he's undrowned
As he that sleeps here swims.

SEBASTIAN   I have no hope   230
That he's undrowned.

ANTONIO   O, out of that no hope
What great hope have you! No hope that way is
Another way so high a hope, that even
Ambition cannot pierce a wink° beyond,
But doubt discovery° there.   235
Will you grant with me
That Ferdinand is drowned?

SEBASTIAN   He's gone.

ANTONIO   Then tell me,
Who's the next heir of Naples?

SEBASTIAN   Claribel.

ANTONIO   She that is Queen of Tunis: she that dwells
Ten leagues beyond man's life;° she that from Naples   240
Can have no note°—unless the sun were post;°
The man i' th' moon's too slow—till newborn chins
Be rough and razorable; she that from whom
We all were sea-swallowed, though some cast° again,
And, by that destiny,° to perform an act   245
Whereof what's past is prologue, what to come,
In yours and my discharge.°

SEBASTIAN   What stuff is this? How say you?
'Tis true my brother's daughter's Queen of Tunis;
So is she heir of Naples, 'twixt which regions
There is some space.

ANTONIO   A space whose ev'ry cubit°   250
Seems to cry out "How shall that Claribel
Measure° us back to Naples? Keep in Tunis,
And let Sebastian wake!" Say this were death

soon forgotten

buried

has the profession of councilor

glimpse

distrust what it sees

a lifetime's journey

information   messenger

thrown on shore

(pun on *cast* = throw of dice)

execution*/performance*

about twenty inches

travel over

plicated and his wit active, ensuring close attention. He takes time so that the murder-plan emerges slowly: he alludes to death (ll. 225-26, 229) before proposing it, and seeks at first only for confirmation of the obvious. He then alludes to the crown again (this time in a riddle) and speaks of an absolute ambition: for a moment his words and rhythms are rousing. But then he stops, and after a pause (ll. 235-36) asks for a repetition of what Sebastian has already agreed to. Now he is ready to consider Claribel (l. 238) and once more seeks an easy answer to ensure that Sebastian follows and assents.

The balance between the two conspirators is subtle and can provide a fascinating interplay in their duologue. Antonio, according to Prospero, was "dry... for sway" (I.ii.114) and knew well how to "set all hearts.../To what tune pleased his ear" (I.ii.85-86), and it is he who now takes most risks and seeks to manipulate Sebastian. In contrast, Sebastian says he is controlled by "hereditary sloth" (l. 215) but he has just taken the lead in taunting Gonzalo (note that Antonio proposed the wager, ll. 27-28) and it was he who spoke bluntly to Alonso (ll. 118-30). Several times Sebastian has seen more deeply into matters than others: note lines 151, 160, 186-88, perhaps 85-86 (see commentary), and, with echoes of *Macbeth*, lines 205-07.

If the actors of these two parts do not possess a finesse suitable for the writing, their duologue will seem weak and unproductive. Directors sometimes cut numerous lines, because there is little scope for enlivening the episode with activity if the speech lacks interest: but this is not easy either, because the text is closely written, each thought meshing with its neighbors.

239-50 Antonio's repetitive phrasing in speaking of Claribel, linked with cosmic and familiar imagery, indicates a renewed energy of delivery. He ends with a theatrical and godlike summons—reminiscent of *Macbeth*'s "imperial theme" (I.iii.127-29). He still has not spoken of murder directly, but Sebastian is fully aware of the implications of what has been said.

At first Sebastian makes a show of alarm or incredulity (l. 247), but then plays for time by recapitulation. Like Antonio, he will not disclose more of his own thoughts than is absolutely necessary until he is convinced that he can trust his fellow.

250-61 Antonio is now ready to speak of murder. He rouses Sebastian with a kind of mimicry and then slips in the word "death" as a supposition. With a quick touch of flattery (ll. 255-56), he presses on to

That now hath seized them, why they were no worse
Than now they are. There be that can rule Naples   255
As well as he that sleeps; lords that can prate
As amply and unnecessarily
As this Gonzalo; I myself could make
A chough of as deep chat.° O, that you bore
The mind that I do, what a sleep were this   260
For your advancement! Do you understand me?

SEBASTIAN   Methinks I do.

ANTONIO   And how does your content°
Tender° your own good fortune?

SEBASTIAN   I remember
You did supplant your brother Prospero.

ANTONIO   True:
And look how well my garments sit upon me,   265
Much feater° than before. My brother's servants
Were then my fellows; now they are my men.

SEBASTIAN   But for your conscience.

ANTONIO   Ay sir, where lies that? If 'twere a kibe,°
'Twould put me to my slipper; but I feel not   270
This deity in my bosom. Twenty consciences
That stand 'twixt me and Milan, candied° be they
And melt, ere they molest!° Here lies your brother—
No better than the earth he lies upon,
If he were that which now he's like, that's dead—   275
Whom I with this obedient steel, three inches of it,
Can lay to bed forever; whiles you, doing thus,
To the perpetual wink° for aye might put
This ancient morsel, this Sir Prudence, who
Should not upbraid our course. For all the rest,   280
They'll take suggestion° as a cat laps milk;
They'll tell the clock° to any business that
We say befits the hour.

SEBASTIAN   Thy case, dear friend,
Shall be my precedent. As thou got'st Milan,
I'll come by Naples. Draw thy sword. One stroke   285

talk only of Gonzalo so that no answer is required immediately. He also keeps Sebastian looking at the sleepers as much as possible. The end of the speech is quiet and its simple question loaded: two men are about to trust each other in committing a political assassination.

a jackdaw to chatter as gravely as he

262-67 Sebastian answers in a brief affirmative; probably they are face to face. When pressed for more, he replies by challenging Antonio, who, sensing victory, is now briskly confident.

satisfaction
regard, take care of

As at lines 234-35 and 245-47, there are echoes here of the murder of Duncan in *Macbeth* (I.iii and V.ii, especially); these men are responding to fear as well as to ambition; they see themselves as murderers as well as in the robes of a monarch. The power of this scene in performance depends on the actors showing the need for "absolute trust" (*Macbeth*, I.iv.14) in their voices, their faces and physical beings; fear is in conflict with desire for possession and power.

more trimly

268 A silence before or after Sebastian speaks marks the crisis of trust; it also shows that he is prepared to follow Antonio.

blister on the heel

269-87 Antonio is now more at ease; he knows Sebastian has at least entertained the idea of murder. He accepts the issue of conscience, speaking of it lightly: it makes him no coward (cf. *Hamlet*, III.i.83 and *Richard III*, V.iii.193); he cares for what he can see and feel, not for a mere idea. Such pragmatism was dangerously against all the ideas on which society was founded in Shakespeare's day: Antonio may laugh at his own iconoclasm (his homely comparisons support such a reading), or he may speak precisely and quietly, proud of his ability to make his own terms with life.

sugared, flattered
cause trouble

sleep

At line 273, Antonio directs Sebastian's attention to Alonso, powerless in his sleep, and then neatly and objectively talks about the practicalities of the murder that he has only glanced at hitherto. He makes everything see easy, maintaining a line of cool and denigrating humor. Yet he does not trust his confederate absolutely, since he reserves the more important murder for his own task. He uses further homely comparisons to play on Sebastian's sense of superiority and give an air of security and normality.

temptation
count the strokes of the clock/agree

Now Sebastian unbends, calling Antonio "dear friend" (l. 283). However he also lets him know, without being instructed, that he as "king" will have to pay for this collusion (ll. 285-87). His concluding words are careful: he is testing their mutual trust and his

Shall free thee from the tribute which thou payest,
And I the king shall love thee.

ANTONIO   Draw together.   *[They draw.]*
And when I rear my hand, do you the like,
To fall it on Gonzalo.

SEBASTIAN   O, but one word!°

Enter ARIEL *[invisible] with music and song.*

ARIEL   My master through his art foresees the danger   290
That you, his friend, are in, and sends me forth—
For else his project dies—to keep them living.
(Sings in GONZALO'S *ear.)* While you here do snoring lie,
          Open-eyed conspiracy
                  His time doth take.   295
          If of life you keep a care,
          Shake off slumber, and beware.
                  Awake, awake!

ANTONIO   Then let us both be sudden.°

GONZALO   *[Awaking.]*   Now good angels
Preserve the king!   *[The others awake.]* 300

ALONSO   Why, how now?—Ho, awake!—Why are you drawn?
Wherefore this ghastly looking?

GONZALO   What's the matter?

SEBASTIAN   Whiles we stood here securing° your repose,
Even now, we heard a hollow° burst of bellowing
Like bulls, or rather lions. Did't not wake you?   305
It struck mine ear most terribly.

ALONSO   I heard nothing.

ANTONIO   O, 'twas a din to fright a monster's ear,
To make an earthquake! Sure it was the roar
Of a whole herd of lions.

ALONSO   Heard you this, Gonzalo?

GONZALO   Upon mine honor, sir, I heard a humming,   310
And that a strange one too, which did awake me.

own courage; he is also well aware that "love" carries political implications.

287-98 The stage is absolutely quiet except for the sound of swords leaving scabbards. Antonio takes command, but Sebastian stops him. Perhaps he is concerned about who should have the prime responsibility or initiative—so Antonio's words, when they have completed their unheard discussions, seem to imply (see I. 299). Or, possibly, Ariel's music precedes his entry and causes a "magic" change of purpose at the point of maximum tension. Even if nothing is heard or seen of Ariel until after line 289, his immediate entry may seem to be the unseen cause of Sebastian's second thoughts.

i.e., one thing more

However motivated, a sudden change diverts dramatic action. The music (usually played by unseen persons offstage) is strange (see II. 304-11) and Ariel speaks to Gonzalo with commanding tones not heard before. (But a pun on "dies", line 292, signals his lack of sympathetic feeling; Ariel is lighthearted, even in a human emergency.) His song is arousing, energetic and harsh.

The conspirators either confer throughout the song or are held "spell-stopped" (see V.i.61) until released by Ariel. During the song or immediately afterwards, Ariel may approach each sleeper in turn, releasing his spell.

quick

299-318 The sudden alarm is as frightening for the would-be murderers as for the awakened sleepers (I. 302). Talk of "earthquake," wild beasts and terror (II. 303-11) indicates that the behavior should be pitched high. Alonso provides a contrast to this because he has not "heard" anything (I. 306); his interjection spurs Antonio to fresh excess of description which no one contradicts.

guarding
echoing, sepulchral

The stage is full of movement and engagement. This echoes the alarms of the storm scene (I.i), only this tempest makes no noise, existing only in the minds of the courtiers, in their fear or guilt. As the activity subsides, awareness of a new, unnamed terror prevails, and more swords are drawn.

Alonso's order to move offstage shows that he is still concerned about his "son" (I. 317): he is not obeyed at once. Gonzalo probably crosses himself, still thinking about the "beasts" (I. 318). On a second order they all move off.

I shaked you sir, and cried. As mine eyes opened,
I saw their weapons drawn. There was a noise,
That's verily. 'Tis best we stand upon our guard,
Or that we quit this place. Let's draw our weapons.   315
                                          [They draw.]
ALONSO   Lead off this ground, and let's make further search
For my poor son.

GONZALO   Heavens keep him from these beasts!
For he is, sure, i' th' island.

ALONSO   Lead away.

ARIEL   Prospero my lord shall know what I have done.
So, king, go safely on to seek thy son.   *Exeunt.*   320

Scene ii *Enter* CALIBAN *with a burden of wood. A noise of thunder*
heard.

CALIBAN   All the infections that sun sucks up
From bogs, fens, flats,° on Prosper fall, and make him
By inchmeal° a disease! His spirits hear me,
And yet I needs must curse. But they'll nor pinch,
Fright me with urchin shows,° pitch me i' th' mire,   5
Nor lead me, like a firebrand, in the dark
Out of my way, unless he bid 'em. But
For every trifle are they set upon me;
Sometime like apes that mow° and chatter at me,
And after bite me; then like hedgehogs which   10
Lie tumbling in my barefoot way and mount
Their pricks at my footfall; sometime am I
All wound° with adders, who with cloven tongues
Do hiss me into madness.

                        Enter TRINCULO.

                        Lo, now lo!
Here comes a spirit of his, and to torment me   15

319-20 Ariel is unlikely to be a passive observer. He may point the courtiers in a particular direction. Or he may spell-stop them while he speaks his couplet and then free them with a gesture of dismissal.

As the king and courtiers leave the stage, frightened and wary, Ariel slips out of sight or, more spectacularly, flies into the air, laughing perhaps.

1-17 In Jacobean public theaters thunder was an impressive sound effect that literally shook the wooden structure of the building. Here it follows immediately on the exits from the previous scene, shattering the silence; it is accompanied with lightning (see III.i.16).

Caliban's curse is heard after the thunder, as answer or complement; usually he heaves the great log he bears into the air threateningly. After this only the wind is heard offstage (see l. 19), but it is enough for Caliban to cower in expectation of more punishment. He tells himself that he is overheard and that the slightest thing he does wrong will be punished: so after the rebellious curse he starts recalling nightmarish horrors, hoping that they will not be inflicted. Perhaps he tries to forestall punishment or talks only to keep up his courage. But the thought of Prospero's bidding, stops any hope of escape and he starts enumerating tortures that are increasingly taunting and enveloping. A soliloquy which had started as defiance, angry, cruel, and resolved, concludes with imaginative suffering, crazed, impotent and close to "madness" (l. 14).

At the peak of Caliban's expectation of torture, a silent fool enters at the back of the stage—the dispirited, fearful Trinculo. At once, perhaps comically, Caliban falls flat on the ground, all remnants of courage gone. He pulls a "gaberdine" (l. 35) over his shoulders so that it covers all but his extremities; he trembles and then manages to lie dead-still.

swamps
little by little

goblin sights

pull faces

coiled around

For bringing wood in slowly. I'll fall flat.
Perchance he will not mind° me.   *[Falls on the ground.]*

TRINCULO   Here's neither bush nor shrub to bear° off any weather
at all, and another storm brewing; I hear it sing i' th' wind.
Yond same black cloud, yond huge one, looks like a foul bom-   20
bard° that would shed his liquor. If it should thunder, as it did
before, I know not where to hide my head. Yond same cloud
cannot choose but fall by pailfuls. What have we here, a man or
a fish? Dead or alive? A fish. He smells like a fish; a very
ancient and fishlike smell; a kind of not of the newest Poor   25
John.° A strange fish. Were I in England now, as once I was,
and had but this fish painted,° not a holiday fool there but
would give a piece of silver.° There would this monster make
a man;° any strange beast there makes a man. When they will
not give a doit° to relieve a lame beggar, they will lay out ten   30
to see a dead Indian. Legged like a man—and his fins like arms!
Warm,° o' my troth! I do now let loose my opinion, hold it no
longer. This is no fish, but an islander, that hath lately suffered
by a thunderbolt. *[Thunder.]* Alas, the storm is come again! My
best way is to creep under his gaberdine;° there is no other   35
shelter hereabout. Misery acquaints a man with strange bedfel-
lows. I will here shroud till the dregs° of the storm be past.
                                  [Creeps under CALIBAN's garment.]

              Enter STEPHANO singing, [a bottle in his hand].

STEPHANO   *[Sings.]* I shall no more to sea, to sea,
                      Here shall I die ashore.
This is a very scurvy tune to sing at a man's funeral. Well,   40
here's my comfort.   *Drinks.*
   (Sings.)   The master, the swabber,° the boatswain, and I,
              The gunner, and his mate,
           Loved Mall, Meg, and Marian, and Margery,
              But none of us cared for Kate.   45
              For she had a tongue with a tang,°
              Would cry to a sailor "Go hang!"
           She loved not the savor of tar nor of pitch;
           Yet a tailor might scratch her where'er she did itch.
              Then to sea, boys, and let her go hang!   50
This is a scurvy tune too. But here's my comfort.   *Drinks.*

notice

ward

leather jug

salted hake

(as a sign to attract customers
to a booth at a fair)

(to see this fish)

make a man's fortune/be
taken for a man (wordplay
on *monster*)

smallest coin

(a *fish* would be cold)

cloak

(wordplay on *bombardment*,
lines 20-21)

petty officer in charge of
cleaning decks

sharp edge/twang

18-37 Trinculo wanders wearily around, looking for shelter, complaining and cowering as he observes a huge black cloud above his head. He seems to take some comfort in knowing that he is about to be drenched: the "cloud cannot choose" but afflict him (ll. 22-23). But as he believes he knows what will happen next, he trips over the prostrate Caliban, who shrinks and trembles at his touch, and then lies absolutely still as if hoping to escape notice.

Trinculo stands back in amazement and then fear. Gingerly, he questions, peers, smells, prods and, finally, pronounces, "A fish" (l. 24). If this does not raise a laugh, Caliban will by shrinking still further under his gaberdine.

Trinculo goes on sniffing and commenting, until he see how this may turn to his own advantage; he soon warms to the idea of making his fortune. By "dead Indian" (l. 31), he has regained his courage and starts prodding his "strange beast" (l. 29) with more purpose. Comic business develops easily here as Trinculo slowly comes to recognize a fellow creature. He is about to investigate when another clap of thunder petrifies him (l. 34). He hurriedly takes shelter, pausing only to make his excuse and, usually, to hold his nose and shut his eyes. He attains a definitive shred of proverbial wisdom about "misery" (l. 36)—delivered with emphasis directly to the audience, it raises an inevitable laugh—and then plunges regardless of discomfort under the gaberdine: there is a commotion, and then all is dead still.

As a traditional clown in a play, Trinculo talks directly to the audience in the theater, demonstrating to them and debating for them and with them. So, as Trinculo finds kinship with Caliban, the audience finds itself close to the fool, enjoying both his sad and his superior jokes, and laughing at him, at Caliban and at the storm itself.

38-52 Drunk, raucous and maudlin, Stephano swaggers on singing; and the actor in this role rides on the comic tide already prepared. The words of his first scrap of song invite baleful yet resolute performance. Perhaps Stephano is lachrymose; certainly he is cheering himself up and needs his "comfort" to put death out of his mind (l. 51). The song of Kate also has a desperate note, emphasized by deliberation and cruelty. By this time an audience's willingness to laugh, so strong at Stephano's entry, may have been entirely quenched; if it has survived it will be in a different, perhaps diffident, spirit.

When Stephano drinks at the end of line 51, he usually sits down on Caliban-Trinculo, thinking the lump to be a rock or mound. As it scuttles, crabwise,

CALIBAN   Do not torment me! O!

STEPHANO   What's the matter? Have we devils here? Do you put
tricks° upon's with savages and men of Inde, ha? I have not
'scaped drowning to be afeared now of your four legs. For it   55
hath been said, "As proper a man as ever went on four legs°
cannot make him give ground";° and it shall be said so again,
while Stephano breathes at'° nostrils.

CALIBAN   The spirit torments me. O!

STEPHANO   This is some monster of the isle with four legs: who   60
hath got, as I take it, an ague.° Where the devil should he
learn our language? I will give him some relief, if it be but for
that. If I can recover° him, and keep him tame, and get to
Naples with him, he's a present for any emperor that ever
trod on neat's leather.°   65

CALIBAN   Do not torment me, prithee. I'll bring my wood home
faster.   *Caliban as Really oblivion*

STEPHANO   He's in his fit now, and does not talk after the wisest.
He shall taste of my bottle. If he have never drunk wine afore,
it will go near to remove his fit. If I can recover him and keep   70
him tame, I will not take too much for him.° He shall pay
for him that hath him, and that soundly.

CALIBAN   Thou dost me yet but little hurt. Thou wilt anon;° I
know it by thy trembling.° Now Prosper works upon thee.

STEPHANO   Come on your ways; open your mouth. Here is that   75
which will give language to you, cat.° Open your mouth.
This will shake your shaking, I can tell you, and that soundly. *[Gives* CALIBAN *drink.]* You cannot tell who's your friend.
Open your chaps again.

TRINCULO   I should know that voice. It should be . . . But he is   80
drowned; and these are devils. O defend me!

STEPHANO   Four legs and two voices—a most delicate° monster!
His forward voice now is to speak well of his friend; his back-
ward voice is to utter foul speeches and to detract. If all the
wine in my bottle will recover him, I will help° his ague. Come!   85
*[*CALIBAN *drinks.]* Amen !° I will pour some in thy other mouth.

play jokes, deceive with con-
juring tricks

(adapting the "two legs" of the
proverb)

retreat

at his

fever

cure

cowhide

i.e., no price will be too high
for him

soon

(taken as a sign of possession
by spirits)

(proverbial saying: "ale will
make a cat speak")

ingenious

cure

that's enough

from beneath him, he will fall clumsily in surprise. Alternatively, Caliban has started to tremble at Stephano's approach and now the drunkard focuses bleared attention on him; in the ensuing silence Caliban cries out and simultaneously four legs shoot out from under the gaberdine, all of them rigid with fear.

53-79 Stephano's first reaction is fear of devils, but his innate sense of superiority triumphs. Caliban lies low and Stephano's courage soon rides high with pride in his own survival; no longer he is "afeared" (l. 55). He sees himself as a valiant knight adventurer. At line 58, he probably prods the monster, which immediately crawls away with ungainly speed or gets suddenly very small as both sufferers cling together in fear beneath the gaberdine. As Caliban cries out in pain (l. 59), Stephano stands back astonished.

By line 60, the monster is trembling violently, so that Stephano thinks it has a fever. Slowly the drunken butler tries to think things through. When it dawns on him that the monster speaks his own "language", he thinks of the devil again, but any fear is banished when he sees his own fortune being made by exploitation—and with that Caliban cries out again, hearing the voice of a master (ll. 66-67).

Stephano thinks quickly now, anxious not to lose his booty: with magnanimity born of avarice, he starts to offer his "bottle" (l. 69); but seeking to "remove his fit" is only the first step of keeping him "tame" and then selling him.

Caliban may speak lines 73-74 to Trinculo, who is shivering with fear, or to Stephano who is struggling to find the mouth of his four-legged monster; or he may not be able to distinguish one from the other, or from his own growing fear of persecution which is heightened by hearing talk of paying "soundly" (l. 72).

Drink silences and stills Caliban at once, and his mouth soon gapes for more.

80-86 While Caliban is drinking, Trinculo's head emerges briefly, for the first time since line 37. But he cannot see Stephano, who is busy tending the monster, so he loses the little confidence he had, panics, and, after one wild look, withdraws totally. At just this moment, Stephano realizes that he is hearing something new; the idea registers and he starts to work out its consequences: capturing the monster will be even more profitable than he had thought, and so again he plies the bottle.

Caliban drinks still more avidly, so that Stephano, with lunatic logic, calls a halt in order to

TRINCULO   Stephano!

STEPHANO   Doth thy other mouth call me? Mercy, mercy! This is
a devil, and no monster. I will leave him; I have no long
spoon.°   90

TRINCULO   Stephano! If thou beest Stephano, touch me, and speak
to me; for I am Trinculo—be not afeared—thy good friend,
Trinculo.

STEPHANO   If thou beest Trinculo, come forth. I'll pull thee by the
lesser legs. If any be Trinculo's legs, these are they. *[Draws*   95
him out from under CALIBAN'*s garment.]* Thou art very Trinculo
indeed! How cam'st thou to be the siege° of this mooncalf?°
Can he vent Trinculos?

TRINCULO   I took him to be killed with a thunderstroke. But art
thou not drowned, Stephano? I hope now thou art not   100
drowned. Is the storm overblown? I hid me under the dead
mooncalf's gaberdine for fear of the storm. And art thou living, Stephano? O Stephano, two Neapolitans 'scaped!

STEPHANO   Prithee do not turn me about; my stomach is not con-
stant.   105

CALIBAN   *[Aside]* These be fine things, and if they be not sprites.
That's a brave god, and bears celestial liquor.
I will kneel to him.

STEPHANO   How didst thou 'scape? How cam'st thou hither?
Swear by this bottle how thou cam'st hither. I escaped upon 110
a butt of sack, which the sailors heaved o'erboard—by this
bottle, which I made of the bark of a tree with mine own
hands since I was cast ashore.

CALIBAN   I'll swear upon that bottle to be thy true subject, for the
liquor is not earthly.   115

STEPHANO   Here! Swear then how thou escap'dst.

TRINCULO   Swum ashore, man, like a duck. I can swim like a duck,
I'll be sworn.

STEPHANO   Here, kiss the book. *[Gives him drink.]* Though thou
canst swim like a duck, thou art made like a goose.   120

Caliban makes an ass
of himself

keep some equality in the administration of his taming liquor, between one mouth and the "other" (86).

(proverbially a necessary utensil for supping with the Devil)

87-98 As Stephano approaches, Trinculo calls loudly and now it is Stephano who is terrified and ready to bolt. With "Mercy, mercy!" all three are petrified and an abruptly serious climax almost parts the comic trio.
Consternation ensues under the gaberdine, all four legs flailing about wildly. Trinculo cries desperately for help and recognition (ll. 91-93), but cannot get out of his shelter, or has not the courage to do so. A comic struggle follows until the two Neapolitans, shaking and puffing, stand facing one another. Caliban curls up into the smallest possible space.

excrement mishapen creature (thought to be malformed at birth due to the moon's influence)

99-103 Trinculo is terrified: the dead monster had proved very much alive, but now he may be facing a ghost. He cannot believe that the thunder has stopped. He tries to explain, doubts his eyes once more, and then staggers forward to touch Stephano. Reassured, he dances jubilantly around with him (see "do not turn me about," l. 104).

104-08 As Stephano steadies himself and Trinculo, Caliban emerges from hiding: in a wholly contrasting tone of naive simplicity and awe (and in verse), he recognizes a new god. He begins to crawl humbly (and perhaps a little drunkenly) towards Stephano.

109-20 Recovering his composure, Stephano starts interrogating and issuing orders. He uses his bottle as a symbol of power and authority, and he forgets his interest in Trinculo's survival to boast of his own exploits. (His manufacture of a bottle is an unlikely exploit; perhaps it is patently untrue.) Caliban instinctively recognizes the power bestowed by Stephano's bottle (l. 114-15); but no one pays attention to him when Stephano is more concerned to dominate Trinculo who has become silent in astonishment, suspicion or fear. He offers the bottle again, but withholds enjoyment until Trinculo has explained himself. Seeing what is required, Trinculo boasts happily in his own fashion, and then drinks contentedly.
Stephano, who cannot swim (see ll. 110-11), denigrates Trinculo's achievement by calling him a fool ("goose," l. 120). He is now master of the situation with two persons—a monster and a fool—subservient to him: he is the new "king" of the island, and a brutal one.
(Stephano's sovereignty does not become explicit until III.ii.101 and IV.i.214, 220-24, but already he is conforming to other images of rule in

TRINCULO   O Stephano, hast any more of this?

STEPHANO   The whole butt, man. My cellar is in a rock by th' sea-
side, where my wine is hid. How now mooncalf, how does
thine ague?

CALIBAN   Hast thou not dropped from heaven?   125

STEPHANO   Out o' th' moon, I do assure thee. I was the Man i' th'
Moon when time was.°

CALIBAN   I have seen thee in her, and I do adore thee. My mistress showed me thee, and thy dog, and thy bush.°

STEPHANO   Come, swear to that; kiss the book. I will furnish it 130
anon° with new contents. Swear.   *[CALIBAN drinks.]*

TRINCULO   By this good light, this is a very shallow monster! I
afeared of him? A very weak monster! The Man i' th' Moon?
A most poor credulous monster! Well drawn,° monster, in
good sooth.   135

CALIBAN   I'll show thee every fertile inch o' th' island; and I will
kiss thy foot. I prithee, be my god.

TRINCULO   By this light, a most perfidious and drunken monster!
When the god's asleep, he'll rob his bottle.

CALIBAN   I'll kiss thy foot. I'll swear myself thy subject.   140

STEPHANO   Come on then: down, and swear!

TRINCULO   I shall laugh myself to death at this puppy-headed
monster. A most scurvy monster! I could find in my heart to
beat him—

STEPHANO   Come, kiss.   145

TRINCULO   But that the poor monster's in drink. An abominable
monster!

CALIBAN   I'll show thee the best springs; I'll pluck thee berries;
I'll fish for thee, and get thee wood enough.
A plague upon the tyrant that I serve!   150
I'll bear him no more sticks, but follow thee,
Thou wondrous man.

the play—Prospero's over Caliban, Miranda and
Ferdinand, and descriptions of Caliban alone on the
island and of Gonzalo in an imaginary Golden Age.)

121-31 Stephano withdraws the bottle and, as
Trinculo eyes it, he asserts that it can be replenished
from a source known only to himself. He turns to
Caliban, leaving Trinculo to digest what he has said.
When Caliban answers in great awe and kneels
in homage, the drunken butler rises easily into a fantasy of his own importance. For Caliban this is no
less than truth, so Stephano rewards his eager ado-
ration with more liquor, assuming a royal benevo-
lence while insisting on obedience.

once upon a time

(the Man in the Moon was
said to have been banished
there with his dog for gathering brushwood on a
Sunday)
soon

drunk

132-47 While Trinculo comments dryly and laughs,
Caliban drinks again and then pauses to offer service
to Stephano, groveling before him, begging him to be
his "god" (l. 137). Trinculo continues to laugh almost
helplessly (see "to death," l. 142): he does not realize
that Stephano's coercive power might be turned
against himself, but happily considers becoming a
tyrant himself to "beat" the "poor monster" (ll. 144,
146). Stephano is silent at first, drawn deeply into his
fantasy-role of tyrant; his posture and face change,
and when he next speaks he is curt, unfeeling and
demanding (ll. 141, 145). Caliban submits to ignomy
and new servitude, kissing Stephano's foot. This
action is absurd and pathetic, and potentially dangerous. (It also shows Shakespeare's continuous concern in this play with servitude and freedom.)

148-64 Caliban offers service, cursing Prospero and
hailing his new tyrant as a wonder. He is transformed
by hope of a new life, not matter what secrets he has
to give up again (compare I.ii.339-40) or what patient
tasks he has to do. In serving this master, his "burden" of "logs" (see II.ii.S.D. and III.i.10) would be as
mere "sticks" (l. 151).
Stephano accepts this worship silently, oblivious of Trinculo's comments; he, too, is transformed,
assuming ever-grander postures of majesty, and
probably drinking noisily.
Caliban responds with still more eager vows,
offering ever more delicate food in tribute. A return to
verse means that in performance his words have precise and delicate effect, and an underlying sustaining
force. The play's action is held back, at its first big
comic climax, while the audience responds to the
imagination of a willing and careful servant whom
Prospero had dismissed earlier as "A freckled whelp,

TRINCULO   A most ridiculous monster, to make a wonder of a
poor drunkard.

CALIBAN   I prithee let me bring thee where crabs° grow;   155
And I with my long nails will dig thee pignuts,°
Show thee a jay's nest, and instruct thee how
To snare the nimble marmoset. I'll bring thee
To clust'ring filberts, and sometimes I'll get thee
Young scamels° from the rock. Wilt thou go with me?   160

STEPHANO   I prithee now, lead the way without any more talking.
Trinculo, the king and all our company else being drowned,
we will inherit here. Here, bear my bottle, fellow Trinculo!
We'll fill him° by and by again.

CALIBAN   *(Sings drunkenly.)* Farewell, master! Farewell, farewell!   165

TRINCULO   A howling monster! A drunken monster!

CALIBAN   *[Sings.]* No more dams° I'll make for fish,
Nor fetch in firing
At requiring,
Nor scrape trenchering,° nor wash dish.   170
'Ban, 'Ban, Cacaliban
Has a new master—get a new man!
Freedom, high-day!° High-day, freedom! Freedom, high-day,
freedom!

STEPHANO   O brave monster! Lead the way.   *Exeunt.* 175

hagborn—not honored with / A human shape"
(I.ii.285-86).

crab apples

ground nuts

By line 161, Stephano is complete king in his
own thoughts. He has emptied the bottle (see l. 164)
and so he orders—probably in all seriousness—a
royal procession of three fools to line up for departure.

165-75   Caliban virtually explodes in pleasure, a
howling, drunken acclamation of freedom. Toward
the end of his revolutionary song, at line 171, he stut-
ters as if relapsing to the "brutish" speech that used
to be all his language (see I.ii.356-60). The royal procession becomes a rout, Stephano loudly assuming
command.

sea gulls (?)

Sometimes Caliban brandishes the huge log he
had carried on at the beginning of the scene (in
accordance with an original stage-direction and in
anticipation of Ferdinand's entry in the scene immediately following). He would raise it now in joyous
exultation, and so the last visual impression of this
communal celebration in the name of "freedom"
might also suggest violence.

i.e., the bottle

However played, this moment provides the
most concerted action since the very beginning of the
play when everyone on shipboard believed they
would drown. The climax is all the more powerful by
contrast with the varied and uncertain actions that
closed the previous scenes. Yet it has come about
without the exercise of Prospero's magic, beyond
that of the storm which falls on all indifferently and
has spent its force near the beginning of the scene.
The key factor in drawing to this conclusion is
Stephano's will to power, operating on the fears and
weaknesses of the others.

(for catching fish)

trenchers, wooden platters

holiday

ACT III

Scene i   *Enter* Ferdinand, *bearing a log.*

FERDINAND   There be some sports are painful, and their labor
Delight in them sets off.° Some kinds of baseness
Are nobly undergone, and most poor matters
Point to rich ends. This my mean° task
Would be as heavy to me as odious, but   5
The mistress which I serve quickens° what's dead,
And makes my labors pleasures. O, she is
Ten times more gentle than her father's crabbed,
And he's composed of harshness. I must remove
Some thousands of these logs and pile them up,   10
Upon a sore injunction.° My sweet mistress
Weeps when she sees me work, and says such baseness
Had never like executor. I forget;°
But these sweet thoughts do even refresh my labors,
Most busy least,° when I do it.

Enter Miranda, *and* Prospero *[behind, unseen].*

MIRANDA   Alas, now pray you,   15
Work not so hard! I would the lightning had
Burnt up those logs that you are enjoined to pile.
Pray set it down, and rest you. When this burns,
'Twill weep for having wearied you. My father
Is hard at study; pray now rest yourself.   20
He's safe for these three hours.

FERDINAND   O most dear mistress,
The sun will set before I shall discharge
What I must strive to do.

MIRANDA   If you'll sit down,
I'll bear your logs the while. Pray give me that;
I'll carry it to the pile.

FERDINAND   No precious creature,   25
I had rather crack my sinews, break my back,

1-15 Ferdinand's entry with a log echoes Caliban's in the previous scene and its manner contrasts with Caliban's exit immediately before. But there is no thunder and no curse.

Usually Ferdinand has stripped off his doublet and is disheveled and dirty; he may look more like Caliban in this servitude than had seemed conceivable.

the trouble they cause makes the pleasure they give seem greater

lowly

Setting down his log, Ferdinand tries to justify the "baseness" (l. 2) of his task, short sentences suiting delivery between deeply-drawn breaths as he recovers from his exertions. As soon as he remembers the "rich ends" for which he works, his vitality

gives life to

"quickens" (l. 6), and his rhythm and phrasing lengthen. Even thoughts of Prospero's "harshness" reminds him of Miranda and he pictures her in his mind, remembering her loving words (ll. 11-13). He has to force himself to return to his "labors". At line 15, he again picks up the heavy log—and at this moment Miranda runs in. He turns to face her and

harsh directive

stands holding the log, forgetting its weight completely.

i.e., my task

Both characters have awoken to a wholly unexpected experience. Surrounded with strange sounds on a mysterious island, made impotent by magic,

busiest when most idle (because occupied with thoughts of love)

encountering a seeming goddess and a harsh, unreasonable father, believing his own father drowned, Ferdinand nevertheless trusts his own feelings and sense of delight, beyond all ordinary discretion. Miranda, in a moment's recognition, has grown from girl to woman and has confronted her protective father to identify boldly with Ferdinand; she knows that she would use Prospero's control of the "lightning" (l. 16) very differently, and she has just escaped, as she thinks, from his surveillance for "three hours" (l. 21).

15-31 While Miranda goes to Ferdinand, Prospero stands at some distance behind her. He may be on an upper level of the stage, as the stage-direction indicates for III.iii.17; but if he is on the same level as the two lovers, the actor will be more able to show his reactions to them and his effort, perhaps, to prevent himself interfering with what happens.

Ferdinand forgets he is holding the log, and when Miranda tells him to "set it down" (l. 18) he does not do so, perhaps because he refuses to seem weak in her eyes or unwilling to serve for her sake. After twice being asked to "rest", Ferdinand apologizes, with utmost reverence, and probably starts work once more.

Usually the log is so huge that Miranda's offer to "bear" it (l. 24) is absurd (her phrases are short, as if

Than you should such dishonor undergo
While I sit lazy by.

MIRANDA   It would become me
As well as it does you; and I should do it
With much more ease, for my good will is to it,   30
And yours it is against.

PROSPERO *[Aside]*   Poor worm, thou art infected;
This visitation° shows it.

MIRANDA   You look wearily.

FERDINAND   No, noble mistress, 'tis fresh morning with me
When you are by at night. I do beseech you—
Chiefly that I might set it in my prayers—   35
What is your name?

MIRANDA   Miranda.—O my father,
I have broke your hest° to say so!

FERDINAND   Admired° Miranda!°
Indeed the top of admiration, worth
What's dearest to the world. Full many a lady
I have eyed with best regard,° and many a time   40
Th' harmony of their tongues hath into bondage
Brought my too diligent° ear. For several° virtues
Have I liked several women; never any
With so full soul but some defect in her
Did quarrel with the noblest grace she owed,°   45
And put it to the foil.° But you, O you,
So perfect and so peerless, are created
Of every creature's best.

MIRANDA   I do not know
One of my sex; no woman's face remember,
Save, from my glass, mine own. Nor have I seen   50
More that I may call men than you, good friend,
And my dear father. How features are abroad,
I am skilless° of; but by my modesty,
The jewel in my dower, I would not wish
Any companion in the world but you;   55
Nor can imagination form a shape,
Besides yourself, to like of. But I prattle

she is preparing to take the strain); and Ferdinand's refusal to say as much is ostentatiously gallant—he does, however, point out that he is under some strain himself. It is hard to know whether Miranda sees the joke in saying that the labor would "become" her (l. 28), but her point about good, or free, "will" is shrewd, because he and not she has been ordered to do the work. By line 31, Ferdinand has put down the log.

When Prospero hears Miranda explain how she has made sure her father is "safe" for three hours (l. 21), he may step forward instinctively, or smile ironically; some Prosperos might turn away as if struggling to hold back from a confrontation.

visit (to Ferdinand)/attack of the plague/act of God

31-32 Prospero's aside points the comedy. He may laugh in good humor, but he speaks of love as a sickness and so he could remain aloof from the feelings of the two young people, counting himself superior. At the other extreme, he could speak as if trying to devalue what he sees, being envious of it and knowing it to be beyond his own competence (see l. 92).

bidding

to be wondered at   (L., *won-derful*)

attention, affection

heedful   different

possessed
overthrow it/offset it

32-59 As Miranda sympathizes, Ferdinand, forgetting his weariness, asserts the ideal nature of his love. He begs to be told her name, with an excuse to show that he is not being presumptuous. Miranda answers impulsively, but instantly remembers her father's prohibition and probably draws back.

Ferdinand echoes her name, accepting it as a token both of trust and wonder. His whole "world" (l. 39) is revalued and, rather clumsily and at some length, he goes on to share his sense of the pettiness of all the women to whom he had previously paid attention. Perhaps he knows that he is saying too much and too little: he breaks off to exclaim on Miranda's perfection.

Miranda replies artlessly, speaking from her "imagination" (l. 56), with words tumbling out "something too wildly" (l. 58). She begins by admitting her contrasting inexperience, but so confidently that she links her new "good friend" with her "dear father", disregarding now the latter's opposition to Ferdinand and his denigration of her good opinion of him in I.ii. As she speaks of "modesty", her thoughts are also running on the "dower" to be given at her wedding. She tells Ferdinand that he is all she longs for, in mind and in body (see "shape", l. 56). By line 57, she has nothing left to say; she probably gazes at Ferdinand and then withdraws a little, aware once more of her father. Both lovers seem foolish at times in this encounter, but comedy need not confuse or mask the delicacy, strength, rapture and transforming nature of their feelings.

ignorant

Something too wildly, and my father's precepts
I therein do forget.

FERDINAND   I am, in my condition,°
A prince, Miranda; I do think a king—   60
I would not so—and would no more endure
This wooden° slavery than to suffer
The fleshfly blow° my mouth. Hear my soul speak:—
The very instant that I saw you, did
My heart fly to your service; there resides,   65
To make me slave to it; and for your sake
Am I this patient log-man.

MIRANDA   Do you love me?

FERDINAND   O heaven, O earth, bear witness to this sound,
And crown what I profess with kind event°
If I speak true! If hollowly,° invert   70
What best is boded me to mischief!° I,
Beyond all limit of what else i' th' world,
Do love, prize, honor you.

MIRANDA   I am a fool
To weep at what I am glad of.

PROSPERO   *[Aside]*   Fair encounter
Of two most rare affections! Heavens rain grace   75
On that which breeds between 'em.

FERDINAND   Wherefore weep you?

MIRANDA   At mine unworthiness, that dare not offer
What I desire to give, and much less take
What I shall die to want.° But this is trifling;
And all the more it seeks to hide itself,   80
The bigger bulk it shows. Hence, bashful cunning,
And prompt me, plain and holy innocence!
I am your wife, if you will marry me;
If not, I'll die your maid. To be your fellow°
You may deny me; but I'll be your servant,   85
Whether you will or no.

FERDINAND   My mistress, dearest,
And I thus humble ever.

59-74 Ferdinand prepares to make a vow. He is thoughtful and sober, speaking of his inheritance without boasting and of his pride without implying that it is important. He calls her by her name, but does not use the word "love"; and claims to serve her, but not assuming acceptance. He hesitates only to speak of his father's death, and then to assure her that it is his "soul" that is engaged (l. 63).

rank

In reply, Miranda asks for love simply, without artifice or cautioning thought (l. 67). With a still more solemn, but more eager vow, Ferdinand pledges life. Before he has finished speaking, Miranda is weeping for joy: her feelings almost overwhelm her, so that in words she can only acknowledge that she is a "fool" (ll. 73-74), unable to express herself.

inferior/log-bearing
contaminate

At line 68, Ferdinand probably kneels, and Miranda may too.

74-76 Prospero's second aside is wholly different from his first. He speaks in joy and admiration, and prays devoutly for the future. His nature, in any performance, will be clearly expressed at this point: does he move towards them, or turn away, or seem most concerned to pray for Heaven's help? How sure is he of their happiness, how much does he share in it? Almost certainly he does not spell-stop the lovers here.

happy ending
falsely
turn to disaster the best that
Fortune has in store for me

77-91 As Ferdinand shows his sympathy and puzzlement, Miranda tries to speak of her love. In a complicated way she tries to explain why she weeps, but very quickly she acknowledges that this is "trifling" and "bashful cunning" (ll. 79-81). She decides to be more direct and offers herself as "wife", before he has asked (l. 83). Any alternative will leave her love unaltered; her fears of rejection tell her this—and she expresses these too. All these thoughts press hard, one after other.

lack

Ferdinand answers simply, insisting still on his "humble" service. It is Miranda who uses the word "husband" first (l. 87), as she had introduced "wife." The incomplete verse-line (l. 88) indicates a pause— whether of wonder, pleasure or disbelief—before Ferdinand's "Ay." He goes on to say that giving his hand in bond of marriage is release and freedom. They both pledge their faiths, probably kneeling together in a formal betrothal. It is a delicate and unruffled climax to the scene: inner content gives new strength and stability to words, and everything is still, including Prospero at some distance. Nothing so far in the play has established such a sense of peace and fulfillment.

equal

MIRANDA   My husband then?

FERDINAND   Ay, with a heart as willing
  As bondage e'er of freedom.° Here's my hand.°

MIRANDA   And mine, with my heart in't. And now farewell,   90
  Till half an hour hence.

FERDINAND   A thousand thousand!°
                      *Exeunt [*FERDINAND *and* MIRANDA *in different directions].*
PROSPERO   So glad of this as they I cannot be,
  Who are surprised withal;° but my rejoicing
  At nothing can be more. I'll to my book;°
  For yet, ere suppertime, must I perform   95
  Much business appertaining.   *Exit.*

Scene ii   *Enter* CALIBAN, STEPHANO, *and* TRINCULO.

STEPHANO   Tell not me! When the butt is out,° we will drink
  water; not a drop before. Therefore bear up and board 'em.
  Servant monster, drink to me.

TRINCULO   Servant monster? The folly of this island! They say
  there's but five upon this isle; we are three of them. If th'   5
  other two be brained like us, the state totters.

STEPHANO   Drink, servant monster, when I bid thee. Thy eyes are
  almost set° in thy head.

TRINCULO   Where should they be set° else? He were a brave monster indeed if they were set in his tail.   10

STEPHANO   My man-monster° hath drowned his tongue in sack.
  For my part, the sea cannot drown me. I swam, ere I could
  recover the shore, five-and-thirty leagues off and on. By this
  light, thou shalt be my lieutenant, monster, or my standard.°

TRINCULO   Your lieutenant, if you list;° he's no standard.°   15

STEPHANO   We'll not run,° Monsieur Monster.

TRINCULO   Nor go neither; but you'll lie° like dogs, and yet say°
  nothing neither.

as ever a slave is to be free
(as a bond of betrothal)

(farewells)

at it
(of magic)

empty
bring (the ship) into the wind
and fight/drink up

closed

placed

servant-monster

standard-bearer

please/lean to one side   he
can't stand, he's drunk

retreat (pun on *stand*)

lie down/excrete (pun on *run*
= urinate)   (pun on *lie* =
tell falsehoods)

But then, with no preparation or explanation, Miranda says "farewell" (l. 90); she probably runs off and Ferdinand calls after her. She may kiss him, and he respond with many more; but the change of mood from the betrothal seems more sudden and sharp than this would imply. Both are radiant with happiness, but break off their meeting rapidly, almost as if afraid to continue together, or as if summoned by another force. Possibly Prospero has exerted his power (as he did at the end of I.ii) and they have become, almost comically, something like robots doing his bidding. Ferdinand takes up his log without another word.

92-96 Prospero does not speak until the lovers have parted. He has been thinking of himself, as well as of them, and so there may be some irony in speaking of his "book" and "business", especially if Ferdinand can still be seen dragging his log offstage. It is a quiet understated and lonely end to the scene.

Prospero is not seen at this moment to be all-powerful, even though his plans are being successful; he must work, to conform to a specific timetable which he has not chosen (see l. 95).

1-22 The comic trio returns, obviously drunk and at cross purposes. Stephano has been playing the role of tyrant, and now adds that of heroic athlete and soldier (ll. 12-14). Trinculo, however, is happy, enjoying their folly and his own; he probably laughs either at Stephano's pronouncements or at his own jokes; or he may giggle most of the time sometimes mirthlessly. Caliban is silent, not through drink, as Stephano supposes, but because he is biding his time to ensure the death of Prospero (see ll. 35-36, 39).

Stephano probably enters supported by Caliban and then collapses onto the stage (see ll. 6, 15, 17, etc.); he then concentrates his attention on getting his "man-monster" to do his bidding and bear him company. Caliban heeds neither drink nor promises, so that Stephano has to insist on his response. Trinculo is ignored by the other two at first and so he comments to the audience or to himself.

Told to speak "but once" in his life (l. 19), Caliban starts to crawl toward his new master to kiss his foot—it is this that had won acceptance before. He pauses to decry Trinculo (ll. 21-22) whose laughter has been an affront to him from the start of the scene.

Line 62 suggests that by this time each of them has been provided with a bottle; in which case they may stand or sit at a greater distance from each other and be more independent than previously.

STEPHANO   Mooncalf, speak once in thy life, if thou beest a good
mooncalf.   20

CALIBAN   How does thy honor? Let me lick thy shoe. I'll not serve
him; he is not valiant.

TRINCULO   Thou liest, most ignorant monster; I am in case° to jos-
tle a constable. Why, thou deboshed° fish thou, was there
ever man a coward that hath drunk so much sack° as I today?   25
Wilt thou tell a monstrous° lie, being but half a fish and half
a monster?

CALIBAN   Lo, how he mocks me! Wilt thou let him, my lord?

TRINCULO   "Lord" quoth he? That a monster should be such a natural!°   30

CALIBAN   Lo, lo again! Bite him to death, I prithee.

STEPHANO   Trinculo, keep a good tongue in your head. If you
prove a mutineer—the next tree!° The poor monster's my
subject, and he shall not suffer indignity.

CALIBAN   I thank my noble lord. Wilt thou be pleased to hearken   35
once again to the suit° I made to thee?

STEPHANO   Marry,° will I, Kneel and repeat. I will stand, and so
shall Trinculo.

Enter ARIEL, *invisible.*

CALIBAN   As I told thee before, I am subject to a tyrant,
A sorcerer that by his cunning hath   40
Cheated me of the island.

ARIEL   Thou liest.

CALIBAN   Thou liest, thou jesting monkey thou.
I would my valiant master would destroy thee.
I do not lie.

STEPHANO   Trinculo, if you trouble him any more in's tale, by this   45
hand, I will supplant° some of your teeth.

TRINCULO   Why, I said nothing.

STEPHANO   Mum° then, and no more. Proceed.

fit
depraved
white wine
huge/malformed

congenital idiot (pun on *monster* = un*natural* creature)

i.e., you will be hanged

request

indeed (originally "by the
Virgin Mary")

uproot

silence

23-41 Trinculo takes issue with Caliban, growing
more valiant himself as he watches Stephano receiv-
ing homage. Caliban does not answer, but appeals to
his new "lord" (l. 28); when he gets no reply, he proceeds to suggest biting his assailant "to death", as if
they were animals. Stephano, seeing his authority
questioned, musters all his dignity to threaten
Trinculo with hanging and to claim Caliban as his
"subject" (ll. 33-34). The fool stops laughing at once,
genuinely frightened. In the silence, Caliban asks for
permission to make his request once more; he
avoids drunken stumbling this time.

Stephano, sensing that his role is at stake,
struggles to his foot and calls Trinculo to attention.
Caliban probably kisses Stephano's foot before
speaking, and while he does so, Ariel enters noise-
lessly—he is invisible to all except the theater audience. The drunken tottering has yielded to comic
solemnity and concentration; as if in a royal presence, Caliban chooses his words, which have added
prominence by a change from prose into verse. He
goes straight to the point.

42-56 A half-line of verse indicates a pause while
Stephano digests what has been said, and then Ariel
intervenes with two simple words. Standing motionless beside Trinculo, he imitates his voice effortless-
ly. Caliban turns angrily and repudiates the charge so
forcibly that the fool is left speechless; a short verse-
line indicates another pause. Stephano turns towards
Trinculo and with ironic politeness threatens physical
violence which he will administer himself. However
he refrains from making an issue of Trinculo's perplexed and, to his ears, inexplicable reply; after a
more familiar reproof, he commands the royal hearing to proceed.

Caliban returns to his cause, repeating twice
more that the island has been taken from him and
pressing on to demand "revenge" (l. 51). He makes
passing reference to Trinculo to flatter his master and

CALIBAN   I say by sorcery he got this isle;
From me he got it. If thy greatness will   50
Revenge it on him—for I know thou dar'st,
But this thing° dare not—

STEPHANO   That's most certain.

CALIBAN   Thou shalt be lord of it, and I'll serve thee.

STEPHANO   How now shall this be compassed?° Canst thou bring   55
me to the party?°

CALIBAN   Yea, yea my lord. I'll yield him thee asleep,
Where thou mayst knock a nail into his head.

ARIEL   Thou liest; thou canst not.

CALIBAN   What a pied° ninny's this! Thou scurvy patch!°   60
I do beseech thy greatness, give him blows
And take his bottle from him. When that's gone,
He shall drink naught but brine, for I'll not show him
Where the quick freshes° are.

STEPHANO   Trinculo, run into no further danger! Interrupt the   65
monster one word further and, by this hand, I'll turn my
mercy out o' doors, and make a stockfish of thee.°

TRINCULO   Why, what did I? I did nothing. I'll go farther off.

STEPHANO   Didst thou not say he lied?

ARIEL   Thou liest.   70

STEPHANO   Do I so? Take thou that. *[Beats* TRINCULO.*]* As you like
this, give me the lie another time.

TRINCULO   I did not give the lie. Out o' your wits, and hearing
too? A pox o' your bottle! This can sack and drinking do. A
murrain° on your monster, and the devil take your fingers!   75

CALIBAN   Ha, ha, ha!

STEPHANO   Now forward with your tale. *[To* TRINCULO*]* Prithee
stand further off.

CALIBAN   Beat him enough. After a little time
I'll beat him too.

at the same time keep the fool in check. Caliban gains Stephano's assent and now offers both his island and his service in return.

Nothing could be more serious or more deeply felt than Caliban's request, and Stephano is entirely caught up in it: as the new king of the island he graciously asks for advice as if murder were an everyday occurrence.

Trinculo says nothing, neither to Caliban's criticism nor to the plan for revenge. He may visibly restrain himself from protest or from laughter; possibly, he is too terrified to speak or move.

57-76 Caliban is delighted and eager. He proposes, as if it were the simplest solution, that Stephano should commit a most brutal murder on the sleeping Prospero.

Again Ariel intervenes with a bare "Thou liest", using Trinculo's voice, adding only "thou canst not" as the bewildered fool turns round to see who has spoken; he moves quickly and easily to keep behind him. The fool stands without a word to say while Caliban mocks him, calls on Stephano to punish him, and promises that he will let Trinculo die for lack of fresh water. Stephano joins in magisterially with a promise to kill Trinculo by beating. Appalled, Trinculo denies doing anything, twice over; and he moves "further off" (l. 68). Stephano however has been challenged and cannot let the matter drop. He bears down on the fool, but before the quarrel develops, Ariel once more intervenes with the same taunting words: and the row precipitates into actual blows. Trinculo runs away, denouncing both of them, and their drinking; but the blows continue and Caliban laughs monstrously.

This episode has ample opportunity for horseplay, but it is also a cartoonlike demonstration of Caliban's concentrated resentment of Prospero and Stephano's insecurity and potential cruelty.

Ariel is easily in command of these very mortal foes: as Stephano lurches toward Trinculo, he stands neatly out of the way; Caliban he infuriates and manipulates.

77-107 Stephano rearranges the royal presence to give audience once more, restraining Caliban and ordering Trinculo still further out of the way.

This time Caliban goes straight to the murderous point, showing by his readiness to list gruesome killings just how fully he has already pondered his

i.e., Trinculo

brought about

person in question

motley, in parti-colored fool/scab

fresh springs

beat you like dried cod is beaten before it is boiled

pestilence

STEPHANO   Stand farther. Come, proceed.   80

CALIBAN   Why, as I told thee, 'tis a custom with him
    I' th' afternoon to sleep. There thou mayst brain° him,
    Having first seized his books; or with a log
    Batter his skull, or paunch° him with a stake,
    Or cut his wezand° with thy knife. Remember   85
    First to possess his books; for without them
    He's but a sot,° as I am, nor hath not
    One spirit to command. They all do hate him
    As rootedly as I. Burn but his books.
    He has brave utensils°—for so he calls them—   90
    Which, when he has a house, he'll deck withal.
    And that most deeply to consider is
    The beauty of his daughter. He himself
    Calls her a nonpareil.° I never saw a woman,
    But only Sycorax my dam and she;   95
    But she as far surpasseth Sycorax
    As great'st does least.

STEPHANO   Is it so brave a lass?

CALIBAN   Ay lord. She will become thy bed, I warrant,
    And bring thee forth brave brood.

STEPHANO   Monster, I will kill this man. His daughter and I will 100
    be king and queen—save our Graces!—and Trinculo and
    thyself shall be viceroys. Dost thou like the plot, Trinculo?

TRINCULO   Excellent.

STEPHANO   Give me thy hand. I am sorry I beat thee; but while
    thou liv'st, keep a good tongue in thy head.   105

CALIBAN   Within this half hour will he be asleep.
    Wilt thou destroy him then?

STEPHANO   Ay, on mine honor.

ARIEL   This will I tell my master.

CALIBAN   Thou mak'st me merry; I am full of pleasure.
    Let us be jocund. Will you troll° the catch°   110
    You taught me but whilere?°

STEPHANO   At thy request, monster, I will do reason,° any

knock out his brains

disembowel
windpipe

fool

fine furnishings

unmatchable in beauty

revenge. He directs particular attention to Prospero's books and, for a moment, sees all the spirits as his potential allies in hatred (II. 88-89). (Some reaction from Ariel is likely here.)

Caliban has now disclosed his plan but Stephano has said nothing yet; so he emphasizes again the need to burn the books as a safety measure. Still there is no response, so he goes on to describe other booty to be captured in the *coup*. Finally he offers Miranda as bait. It costs him a great deal to yield to his new king the very prize for which he had lost Prospero's love (see I.ii.346-53). He is unable to describe her in his own words, so he offers Prospero's. Line 94 is either highly irregular verse, with many syllables crowding into one iambic pentameter, or it is spoken as two half-lines with a long pause between them. All Caliban can add to carry conviction is a recollection of his mother as the only "woman" he has known and to voice his bewildered, hopeless sense of Miranda's infinite superiority.

Stephano is impressed (I. 97) and Caliban follows up this success by offering Miranda again, and promising a "brave brood." After a pause (I. 99), Stephano gives his affirmative decision, striking attitudes of command and calling Trinculo back into royal favor. The fool's "Excellent" (I. 103) can be ironic or thoughtless, or weakly acquiescent. Stephano, now unconscious of criticism, steamrollers forward, commanding all to his own satisfaction. Caliban recalls him to the immediate purpose and is given an oath of committal (I. 107).

Caliban's murderous cruelty, "rooted" in hatred (I. 89), and his rapt evocation of Miranda's beauty both cut against the tide of comedy; he has an imaginative mind that makes its presence felt with speech and silence.

108-17 As Ariel is about to move off (I. 108), Caliban breaks into clumsy good spirits; he may croon or grunt with pleasure. In a three-part song, each singer starting one line after the other, they sing again of freedom, this time linked with derision for their adversaries. But the three are not in agreement about the tune and the singing ends chaotically. In their disarray, Caliban is the one to be worried: he speaks with serious—and, in the circumstances, comic—decisiveness.

sing lustily   round song for
    three or more voices
just now

give satisfaction

118-27   Ariel's playing of the right tune silences everyone. Trinculo tries to laugh it off, but as the music continues he is obviously terrified (I. 123). Stephano, sensing a challenge, responds with defi-

reason.° Come on, Trinculo, let us sing.
(Sings.)   Flout° 'em and scout° 'em,
             And scout 'em and flout 'em: 115
             Thought is free!°

CALIBAN   That's not the tune.
                        ARIEL *plays the tune on a tabor°and pipe.*
STEPHANO   What is this same?

TRINCULO   This is the tune of our catch, played by the picture of
    Nobody.°   120

STEPHANO   If thou beest a man, show thyself in thy likeness. If
    thou beest a devil, take't as thou list.°

TRINCULO   O forgive me my sins!

STEPHANO   He that dies pays all debts.° I defy thee.—Mercy upon
    us!   125

CALIBAN   Art thou afeard?

STEPHANO   No monster, not I.

CALIBAN   Be not afeard; the isle is full of noises,°
    Sounds and sweet airs that give delight and hurt not.
    Sometimes a thousand twangling instruments   130
    Will hum about mine ears; and sometime voices
    That, if I then had waked after long sleep,
    Will make me sleep again; and then, in dreaming,
    The clouds methought would open, and show riches
    Ready to drop upon me, that when I waked,   135
    I cried to dream again.

STEPHANO   This will prove a brave kingdom to me, where I shall
    have my music for nothing.

CALIBAN   When Prospero is destroyed.

STEPHANO   That shall be by and by. I remember the story.   140

TRINCULO   The sound is going away; let's follow it, and after do
    our work.

STEPHANO   Lead monster; we'll follow. I would I could see this
    taborer; he lays it on.°

TRINCULO   Wilt come? I'll follow Stephano.   *Exeunt.* 145

reasonable thing
jeer   mock

(proverbial saying)

small drum (often carried by
   fools)

(both a contemporary title-
page illustration and a sta-
tioner's sign depicted a
trunkless man—all head,
arms, and legs)
(proverb: "the devil take it")

(proverbial consolation)

music, sounds

does it in style/beats (the
   drum) vigorously

ance, but then he, too, becomes terrified. Both are on their knees before something that they can hear but cannot see. Caliban says nothing at all; perhaps he trembles expecting punishment.

When the sprightly tune stops, Caliban is the first to speak and his question forces Stephano to recover some of his bravado.

128-38   Caliban's concern for Stephano is unexpectedly gentle; his master had denied being "afeard," but Caliban can recognize fear when he sees it. To reassure him, he talks of the island's music with great delicacy, his words sustained by gentle and lulling rhythms until he remembers his tears at the loss of all delight (l. 136). There is a pause before Stephano jokes and boasts about his "kingdom", in an attempt to recover their spirits. At the touch of fear, boisterous comedy and ferocious talk have yielded to rapt attention.

Caliban's description of enchantment and dreams is a climactic and effective opportunity for the actor to emphasize the gentler and more responsive aspects of Caliban and his independence. In the structure of the play, it is significant as one of a series of incidents in which characters show the nature and strength of their imaginations. Alonso, Gonzalo, Ferdinand and Miranda have already done so (see II.i.106-08, 138-64; III.i.14, 54-57); Prospero will call for a masque in the next Act to represent his own "present fancies" (IV.i.122) and then liken all human experience to such a dream. The delight, power and insecurity of imaginary "reality" are thus made evident, and also its dangers: Prospero, for example, abruptly ends the masque (see IV.i.139) because he remembers the practical necessity of coping with Caliban's conspiracy.

139-45   Caliban insists on practicalities, calling for violence. When the music is heard again, however, the other two follow it instinctively, no longer afraid. They have survived, and their dazed minds now enjoy the tune without bothering about its source or whether they are sleeping or awake. Stephano is the least impressed, being sure that some "taborer" lays on the music for them. However Caliban is made to go first, just to be sure. He says nothing more, but line 145 suggests that he hesitates before obeying. Trinculo places himself, craftily, in the rear of the procession.

In many productions, the tune sets them singing and dancing before they go out of sight; however, they could still be clinging together for support. Ariel leads the way, amused and in control.

Scene iii   *Enter* ALONSO, SEBASTIAN, ANTONIO, GONZALO, ADRIAN,
FRANCISCO, etc.

GONZALO   By'r Lakin,° I can go no further, sir;
My old bones ache. Here's a maze trod indeed
Through forthrights and meanders.° By your patience,
I needs must rest me.

ALONSO   Old lord, I cannot blame thee,
Who am myself attached° with weariness   5
To th' dulling of my spirits. Sit down and rest.
Even here I will put off my hope, and keep it
No longer for my flatterer. He is drowned
Whom thus we stray to find, and the sea mocks
Our frustrate° search on land. Well, let him go.   10

ANTONIO   *[Aside]* I am right glad that he's so out of hope.
Do not for° one repulse forgo the purpose
That you resolved t' effect.

SEBASTIAN   *[Aside]*   The next advantage°
Will we take throughly.°

ANTONIO   *[Aside]*   Let it be tonight;
For, now they are oppressed with travel, they   15
Will not nor cannot use such vigilance
As when they are fresh.

Solemn and strange music; and PROSPERO *on the top,° invisible. Enter several strange* SHAPES,° *bringing in a banquet; and dance about it with gentle
actions of salutations; and, inviting the king, etc. to eat, they depart.*

SEBASTIAN   *[Aside]*   I say tonight. No more.

ALONSO   What harmony is this? My good friends, hark!

GONZALO   Marvelous sweet music!

ALONSO   Give us kind keepers,° heavens! What were these?   20

SEBASTIAN   A living drollery.° Now I will believe
That there are unicorns; that in Arabia
There is one tree, the phoenix'° throne; one phoenix
At this hour reigning there.

Lady (By Our Lady)

staight and winding paths

1-10 The court party enter tired and disheveled, but staying together in one group so far as they can. Their swords are still drawn. Gonzalo is straggling and calls out for permission to rest; he has to wait until line 6 when he makes himself as comfortable as possible on the ground, taking some time to do so. As the whole party has stopped, Alonso accepts defeat: the "sea," he concludes has taken his son (l. 9). All his grief comes back, but he does not speak of it; "Well, let him go" (l. 10) seems to be as much an instruction to himself as to his courtiers.

seized

    Alonso sits down and the others sheathe their swords and begin to do the same. But Antonio and Sebastian move together and to one side; they speak privately, and remain alert and watchful. For fear of being overheard they refer only generally to what has been "resolved" (l. 13); Sebastian is the more aware of the need for urgency and the fewest possible words (see l. 17).

vain

because of

opportunity
thoroughly

18-20 As music takes over from talk, Alonso and Gonzalo respond at once. But then the "shapes" enter and Alonso's wonder turns to fear; he prays for protection and then is silent. The creatures are each different (see "several kinds," l. 88) and all "monstrous" (31); they say nothing as they bring in the banquet and then dance around it making gestures of greeting and of invitation to the feast. The effect is that of an ocular riddle.

upper stage
apparitions

    At a higher level, Prospero also enters and watches; he is silent so that the audience in the theater is as puzzled as those who are confronted with the spectacle on stage.

guardian angels

puppet show*

(fabulous bird; only one was said to exist at a time, each new one being born out of the ashes of the previous one)

21-42 Antonio and Sebastian are the first to react, possibly because they were caught standing on the entry of the shapes. The unreal seems now to be real to them; and yet to believe what they are seeing, they remember what had seemed unbelievable. It seems impossible, but other people must be the "fools" (l. 27). Their eyes are on the "shapes", not on the banquet; and when Gonzalo joins their debate the point

ANTONIO   I'll believe both;
And what does else want credit,° come to me,   25
And I'll be sworn 'tis true. Travelers ne'er did lie,°
Though fools at home condemn 'em.

GONZALO   If in Naples
I should report this now, would they believe me?
If I should say I saw such islanders—
For certes° these are people of the island—   30
Who, though they are of monstrous shape, yet note,
Their manners are more gentle, kind, than of
Our human generation you shall find
Many—nay, almost any.

PROSPERO   *[Aside]*   Honest lord,
Thou hast said well; for some of you there present   35
Are worse than devils.

ALONSO   I cannot too much muse°
Such shapes, such gesture, and such sound, expressing—
Although they want the use of tongue—a kind
Of excellent dumb discourse.

PROSPERO   *[Aside]*   Praise in departing.°

FRANCISCO   They vanished strangely.

SEBASTIAN   No matter, since   40
They have left their viands behind; for we have stomachs.
Will't please you taste of what is here?

ALONSO   Not I.

GONZALO   Faith sir, you need not fear. When we were boys,
Who would believe that there were mountaineers
Dewlapped° like bulls, whose throats had hanging at 'em   45
Wallets of flesh? Or that there were such men
Whose heads stood in their breasts? Which now we find
Each putter-out of five for one° will bring us
Good warrant of.

ALONSO   I will stand to, and feed;
Although my last, no matter, since I feel   50
The best is past. Brother, my lord the duke,
Stand to, and do as we.

lack belief
(proverbially, travelers were liars)

certainly

wonder at

i.e., don't judge until the end of the entertainment (proverbial)

with loose flesh hanging at the neck

traveler who deposits money to be repaid fivefold if his journey is successful*

at issue becomes the contrast between the "monstrous" shapes (this word has been used repeatedly of Caliban) and their "gentle" behavior: should one trust behavior or appearance, action or being? Uncharacteristically Gonzalo doubts his own credibility and concludes by correcting his own estimate of the world he thought knew thoroughly.

Prospero's asides direct some attention to himself presiding over the spirits and closely watching how they are received; they also underline the moral issues that he hopes the show will raise. On his second, more ominous comment, the shapes suddenly, as "strangely" (l. 40) as everything else has happened in the interlude.

Francisco, who had witnessed to the survival of Ferdinand (II.i.108-17), is the first to comment, but the others move a step ahead concerned now with the banquet that is left temptingly behind and the question that it unambiguously poses. Each response reveals the nature of the speaker: Sebastian thinks of obvious needs and wants to stop mere talk about the strangeness of what has happened. Alonso, at first, emphatically and without reasoning, rejects eating; his unspoken thoughts possess him so fully that Gonzalo thinks he is afraid.

43-52 Gonzalo is surprisingly reassuring; he bypasses the moral riddle and is pleased to argue that since the unbelievable has happened they should be ready for anything. Alonso then sees no reason to resist: he will eat, not because he has thought the case through for himself, but because he is desperate and beyond caring. Having waited for the king to move since line 42, all the courtiers start to follow him towards the banquet—and the trap is sprung.

The spectacle had been a test: they accept food offered by monstrous beings, because they need it, or think it suitable, or because they do not care to do otherwise; for some of them the mere appearance of kindness and civility had been a sufficient recommendation. (Compare the temptation of Christ in the wilderness; *Matthew*, iv.1-10 and *Luke*, iv.1-13.)

This was a crucial decision: each member of the court party now stands still, horrified by the thunder and lightning (an echo of the original tempest of I.i, which had made all souls feel "a fever of the mad," I.ii 210). Then the furious harpy flies down, or rises out of a trap in the stage, and with this miraculous and unexpected movement displaces the banquet.

Harpies (from the Greek *harpyiai*, or snatchers) were associated with the "Furies" of ancient myth, instruments of divine vengeance on mortals, and

Thunder and lightning. Enter ARIEL, *like a harpy;° claps his wings upon
the table and, with a quaint device,° the banquet vanishes.*

ARIEL   You are three men of sin, whom Destiny—
That hath to instrument° this lower world
And what is in't—the never-surfeited sea   55
Hath caused to belch up° you, and on this island
Where man doth not inhabit—you 'mongst men
Being most unfit to live. I have made you mad;
And even with suchlike valor° men hang and drown
Their proper° selves.   *[All draw their swords.]*
                        You fools! I and my fellows   60
Are ministers of Fate. The elements,
Of whom your swords are tempered, may as well
Wound the loud winds, or with bemocked-at stabs
Kill the still-closing° waters, as diminish
One dowle° that's in my plume. My fellow ministers   65
Are like° invulnerable. If° you could hurt,
Your swords are now too massy for your strengths,
And will not be uplifted. But remember—
For that's my business to you—that you three
From Milan did supplant good Prospero;   70
Exposed unto the sea, which hath requit it,°
Him and his innocent child; for which foul deed
The powers, delaying not forgetting, have
Incensed the seas and shores, yea, all the creatures,
Against your peace. Thee of thy son, Alonso,   75
They have bereft; and do pronounce by me
Ling'ring° perdition—worse than any death
Can be at once°—shall step by step attend
You and your ways; whose° wraths to guard you from—
Which here, in this most desolate isle, else falls   80
Upon your heads—is nothing but heart's sorrow
And a clear° life ensuing.

He vanishes in thunder; then, to soft music, enter the SHAPES *again and
dance, with mocks and mows,° and carrying out the table.*

PROSPERO   Bravely° the figure of this harpy hast thou
Performed, my Ariel; a grace it had, devouring.°

half woman, half carion bird;
instrument of divine
vengeance   ingenious
mechanism

as agent

(against its nature)

i.e., the courage of madness

own

continually closing over (self-
 healing)
fine feather
also   even if

repaid the crime

prolonged
at any one time
(referring to *powers*, line 73)

pure

derisive gestures and grimaces

finely

(harpies were voracious)

also with whirlwinds. Homer suggested that they had characteristics of horses, but later in the *Aeneid*, and elsewhere, harpies were filthy, loathsome, horrific and rapacious creatures, half-carrion bird and half-woman. These harpies carried away food from King Phineus of Thrace and excreted on what was left. Virgil says that their faces are pale with hunger, that they could not be wounded and that their stench was foul. Such are the characteristics present in Ariel's disguise; Prospero says he had a "devouring" grace (l. 84) in preventing the banquet being ate and making it disappear.

52-82 Grotesque and quivering, with feathered wings heightening his stature so that he stands high above the table, Ariel now speaks authoritatively, in a measured and complicated style that combines force with precision. His speech is unlike any other so far in the play: it is rich with parentheses and epithets, metrically firm and yet sustained by emphatic rhythms. It is spoken on behalf of "Fate," who is in full control over the "lower world," the elements, and man's motivations and strength of body. The actor needs an unhurried energy, well-controlled breathing and careful preparation; each word must clear and decisive. (Perhaps a well-trained boy-actor in the play's first performances could also have achieved an impersonal severity, appropriate to the spirit who speaks only as an instrument for Prospero.)

His hearers are first made "mad" (l. 58), as they had been on the ship in I.i, and then weak and tongue-tied. They draw their swords only to be incapable of wielding them. Their world has become unfamiliar and terrifying, and yet they hear words that speak directly to their consciences. As Ariel singles out Alonso for a final denunciation and tells a lie, saying that Ferdinand is dead, the king may weep in grief and guilt.

By now all are probably on their knees or lying prostrate, and Ariel concludes with some ray of hope (ll. 79-82), a contrast to the entire speech. Then thunder again shakes the theater. Probably, fireworks and smoke accompany his disappearance, sinking through a trapdoor in the stage or flying off.

83-93 The court party is stunned, the king at least is in a "strange stare" (l. 95). To music (now "soft," rather than "strange and solemn," as before), the spirits re-enter for a taunting dance and to carry out the now-empty table.

Of my instruction hast thou nothing bated°   85
In what thou hadst to say. So, with good life°
And observation° strange, my meaner° ministers
Their several kinds° have done. My high charms work,
And these, mine enemies, are all knit up
In their distractions.° They now are in my power;   90
And in these fits I leave them, while I visit
Young Ferdinand, whom they suppose is drowned,
And his and mine loved darling.   *[Exit above.]*

GONZALO   I' th' name of something holy, sir, why stand you
In this strange stare?°

ALONSO   O, it is monstrous, monstrous!   95
Methought the billows spoke, and told me of it;
The winds did sing it to me; and the thunder,
That deep and dreadful organ pipe, pronounced
The name of Prosper; it did bass° my trespass.
Therefore my son i' th' ooze is bedded; and   100
I'll seek him deeper than e'er plummet sounded,
And with him there lie mudded.   *Exit.*

SEBASTIAN   But one fiend at a time,
I'll fight their legions o'er!°

ANTONIO   I'll be thy second.
                        Exeunt [SEBASTIAN and ANTONIO].
GONZALO   All three of them are desperate. Their great guilt,
Like poison given to work a great time after,   105
Now 'gins to bite the spirits. I do beseech you,
That are of suppler joints, follow them swiftly,
And hinder them from what this ecstasy°
May now provoke them to.

ADRIAN   Follow, I pray you.
                        Exeunt omnes.

omitted

lifelike

attention to detail   inferior
(to Ariel)

individual functions

mad fits, confusion

fixed look of horror

proclaim in deep voice*

to the end

madness

Meanwhile Prospero's speech marks a pivotal point in the play. He has convicted his "enemies" of their crimes and pronounced sentence; he has also called for "heart's sorrow" (l. 81) as the only mitigation of endless and slow torture. Having demonstrated his magic power, his speech rings with confidence and exultation as never before in the play; it reaches two climaxes, on "My high charms work" and "They now are in my power" (ll. 88, 90).

His next step is crucial and taken without hesitation: he leaves his enemies to visit Ferdinand and his "loved" Miranda (l. 93). But he does not say—he may not know—why he leaves the stage; perhaps the spectacle has tried *his* resources too; perhaps he goes to keep control over the young lovers; perhaps he thinks of a restorative future. The half verse-line 93 indicates a pause, so nothing more happens until after Prospero has gone; this ensures that the audience watches him closely and that whatever motivation the actor has discovered for the exit will register fully.

94-109 As Prospero leaves, the spell that has held the court party is broken, but Gonzalo notices that Alonso is still transfixed. He tries to rouse him, but terror continues to possess the king's mind. He cries out at first, unable to shake off the horror (l. 95). But then he begins to recall what he has just experienced. When this gives no relief but rather accentuates his guilt, he rushes out doomed and hopeless, believing the lie which Ariel, on Prospero's instruction, has told him; he leaves in order to drown himself as deep in the sea as he can reach, where he believes his son is "bedded" (l. 100).

Sebastian and Antonio start making "desperate" (l. 104) lunges with their swords, as if fighting, or preparing to fight, with numberless devils. They rush off the stage.

The rest are too frightened to say or do anything until Gonzalo rouses them to follow the three desperate madmen. They delay a moment to beg Gonzalo not to stay behind. The stage is soon empty.

ACT IV

Scene i   *Enter* PROSPERO, FERDINAND, *and* MIRANDA.

PROSPERO   If I have too austerely punished you,
Your compensation makes amends, for I
Have given you here a third of mine own life,
Or that for which I live; who once again
I tender° to thy hand. All thy vexations   5
Were but my trials of thy love, and thou
Hast strangely° stood the test. Here, afore heaven,
I ratify this my rich gift. O Ferdinand,
Do not smile at me that I boast her off,
For thou shalt find she will outstrip all praise,   10
And make it halt° behind her.

FERDINAND   I do believe it
Against an oracle.

PROSPERO   Then, as my gift, and thine own acquisition
Worthily purchased, take my daughter. But
If thou dost break her virgin-knot before   15
All sanctimonious° ceremonies may
With full and holy rite be minist'red,
No sweet aspersion° shall the heavens let fall
To make this contract grow;° but barren hate,
Sour-eyed disdain,° and discord shall bestrew   20
The union of your bed with weeds° so loathly
That you shall hate it both. Therefore take heed,
As Hymen's° lamps shall light you.

FERDINAND   As I hope
For quiet days, fair issue,° and long life,
With such love as 'tis now, the murkiest den,   25
The most opportune place, the strong'st suggestion°
Our worser genius° can,° shall never melt°
Mine honor into lust, to take away
The edge° of that day's celebration,
When I shall think or° Phoebus' steeds° are foundered   30
Or Night kept chained below.

1-32 Prospero leads Ferdinand and Miranda to where "afore heaven" he is to give his daughter formally away in a betrothal ceremony. His opening words and the rhythms of his speech are composed, a complete contrast to the "desperate" actions and "ecstacy" which concluded the previous scene (III.iii.104, 108). Yet Prospero is deeply involved, since Miranda, he says, is "that for which I live" (I. 4): he takes a personal burdened care; at this stage, he thinks of others only in terms of his relationship to them.

offer (pun; *tender* = care for)

wonderfully

At line 5, Ferdinand takes Miranda's hand, and they continue like this until line 32.

The formal betrothal is very quickly concluded (see II. 7-8) and at once Prospero is uncertain whether all has been appropriate: for a moment, the great man of "Art" doubts the effect of what he has accomplished—a new note in the composition of his character, not stressed, indeed struck lightly or humorously, but significant none the less. (Contrast "My foot my tutor", I.II.472).

limp

The short verse-line (I. 12) gives a pause in which the lovers may kiss in token of their mutual "vows" (see I. 96). Then Prospero formally relinquishes his daughter (I. 14)—an act that had been implicit, at least, in his earlier ratification of the "gift" (I. 8); he prolongs this moment now, issuing a solemn warning to his new son. His words have religious implications here, acknowledging both heavenly purity and human corruption. Ferdinand replies with a careful and sustained speech that echoes Prospero's tone but has greater vigor and more particular reference to the facts of living. He concludes with mythical references and heroic and blazing images (II. 30-31).

sacred

blessing (sprinkling of dew)*
become fruitful
aversion, contempt
(instead of the usual flowers)

(god of marriage; he carried a torch)

children

temptation

bad angel   is capable of
(with the heat of desire)

so as to spoil the keen delight
either   horses that draw the
     sun god's chariot

This whole passage needs to be performed carefully. At the start Prospero can appear too apologetic or too patronizing. His insistence that Miranda's virginity is kept until the wedding-night can sound pedantic, otherworldly, puritanical or obsessive—although these interpretations are more common in critical studies than in the theater. Prospero has just left his enemies to visit his "loved darling" (III.iii.88-93), relinquishing his position of power at a higher level above the stage. Implicit in all he says should be Prospero's love for Miranda, as well as his determination to root out evil: he is at once tender, severe, involved and critical; he cares intensely how his plans work out, but he is more aware than before, as he looks at the young lovers, that he cannot assume that what he contrives will have he effect he wishes. He is, perhaps, a little frightened.

PROSPERO   Fairly spoke.
Sit then, and talk with her: she is thine own.
What,° Ariel! My industrious servant, Ariel!

Enter ARIEL.

ARIEL   What would my potent master? Here I am.

PROSPERO   Thou and thy meaner fellows your last service   35
Did worthily perform; and I must use you
In such another trick.° Go bring the rabble,°
O'er whom I give thee power, here to this place.
Incite them to quick motion;° for I must
Bestow upon the eyes of this young couple   40
Some vanity° of mine art. It is my promise,
And they expect it from me.

ARIEL   Presently?°

PROSPERO   Ay, with a twink.°

ARIEL   Before you can say "Come" and "Go,"
And breathe twice, and cry, "So, so,"   45
Each one, tripping on his toe,
Will be here with mop and mow.°
Do you love me, master? No?

PROSPERO   Dearly, my delicate Ariel. Do not approach
Till thou dost hear me call.

ARIEL   Well: I conceive.°   *Exit.* 50

PROSPERO   Look thou be true. Do not give dalliance
Too much the rein; the strongest oaths are straw
To th' fire i' th' blood. Be more abstemious,
Or else good night° your vow.

FERDINAND   I warrant you, sir,
The white cold virgin snow upon my heart   55
Abates the ardor of my liver.°

PROSPERO   Well.
Now come, my Ariel; bring a corollary°
Rather than want° a spirit. Appear, and pertly.°   *Soft music.*
No tongue!° All eyes! Be silent.

come

device   "thy meaner fellows"

activity (pun on = puppet
    show)

show, trifle

immediately

winking of the eye

grins and grimaces

understand

goodbye to

(supposed to be the seat of
    sexual passion)

surplus*

lack   briskly

(silence was necessary for
    magic)

33-34 As Miranda, who has been silent so far in the scene, goes with Ferdinand to sit and talk (see l. 32), Prospero turns away and calls for Ariel. The spirit enters at once, announcing "Here I am" (l. 34) as if Prospero needs assurance. His first "potent" master, and Prospero's instructions have an unfamiliar note of necessity and compulsion: he himself "must" do this and that (36-39), he has made a "promise" (l. 41). Possibly "such another trick" and "vanity of mine art" suggest an equally unusual note of self-criticism or apology. The father's mood is assertive after the loss of his daughter, but not easily so, not confidently.

The demonstrative "this young couple" (l. 40) suggests that Prospero turns in their direction at this point, or a little before. Presumably they are talking together as instructed, or have now fallen silent. Ariel's "Presently?" may indicate that Prospero's thoughts are far away from immediate action by this time, quick to think about what might happen between the two young people.

44-50 Ariel's neat, rhyming doggerel may be accompanied with a "tripping" and sprightly dance; he cannot go about his business because he has not been instructed, but he takes time to demonstrate just how quickly everything will be performed. "Do you love me...?" seems to follow as a contrasting flash of instinctive feeling and concern. But Ariel is said to have no human "affections" (see V.i.18-24), so his question may be merely quizzical or high-spirited. Alternatively, with the following "No?", his query may arise from a continuing sense that his "potent" (l. 34) master is more than usually a constraint upon his freedom; perhaps he had been expecting thanks for his lively promise of attentive work.

Prospero's reply could be deeply touched; it is noticeable that he exchanges "industrious servant" (l. 33) for "delicate Ariel" (l. 49). But it is very brief; assuming that Ariel now knows what to do, Prospero dismisses him until he is required. With his master in this mood, Ariel says very little and leaves the stage with an abruptness contrasting with the playfulness of his song and dance.

51-59 As Ariel flies off, Prospero turns towards the lovers again and is more outspoken than before. In performance, "Be more abstemious" (l. 53) is sometimes a rebuke for embracing too passionately; but if so, Ferdinand's reply sounds unlikely and hypocritical. Prospero may be responding to his encounter with Ariel's free spirit, rather than to the young people, and speaking about his own fears, rather than commenting on what is taking place.

Enter Iris.

Iris   Ceres,° most bounteous lady, thy rich leas°   60
Of wheat, rye, barley, vetches, oats, and peas;
Thy turfy mountains, where live nibbling sheep,
And flat meads° thatched with stover,° them to keep;
Thy banks with pionèd° and twillèd° brims,
Which spongy April at thy hest° betrims   65
To make cold nymphs chaste crowns; and thy broom groves,
Whose shadow the dismissèd° bachelor loves,
Being lasslorn;° thy pole-clipt° vineyard;
And thy sea-marge,° sterile and rocky-hard,
Where thou thyself dost air°—the queen o' th' sky,°   70
Whose wat'ry arch° and messenger am I,
Bids thee leave these, and with her sovereign grace,

Juno *descends.* °

Here on this grass plot, in this very place,
To come and sport;° her peacocks° fly amain.°
Approach, rich Ceres, her to entertain.   75

Enter Ceres.

Ceres   Hail, many-colored messenger, that ne'er
Dost disobey the wife of Jupiter,
Who, with thy saffron wings, upon my flow'rs
Diffusest honey drops, refreshing show'rs,
And with each end of thy blue bow dost crown   80
My bosky° acres and my unshrubbed down,
Rich scarf° to my proud earth. Why hath thy queen
Summoned me hither, to this short-grassed green?

Iris   A contract of true love to celebrate
And some donation freely to estate°   85
On the blessed lovers.

Ceres   Tell me, heavenly bow,°
If Venus or her son,° as thou dost know,
Do now attend the queen? Since they did plot
The means that dusky Dis° my daughter got,

goddess of agriculture   fields

meadows   winter feed for
cattle

trenched* (?)   ridged* (?)

command

rejected

forsaken   lined with poles*
(before new season's
growth)

seacoast

take the air   Juno, wife of
Jupiter

i.e., rainbow

(on slow-moving stage
machine)

enjoy herself   (drawing her
chariot)   in full flight

bushy

adornment, sash

bestow

Iris

Cupid

god of the underworld who
abducted Proserpina, the
goddess of spring

Prospero's one-word and ambiguous reply to Ferdinand (l. 56) suggests that his mind is elsewhere by this time: the masque will speak for him, enacting his "present fancies" (l. 122) and demonstrating his hope of "hourly joys" (l. 108) for the young lovers. When the music begins, he rather brusquely silences Ferdinand and Miranda.

60-75 The rhymed speeches have stately rhythms and ornate descriptions. Rare and new words are used, and the syntax is protracted and varied. The characters address each other formally, varying their titles and listing their attributes. As Ferdinand says later, it is artfully "majestic" and "harmonious" (ll. 118-19). While the flowing, "many-colored" robes and "saffron wings" of Iris attract attention (ll. 76, 78), her opening invocation delights the ear and evokes visual and sensual images in hearers' minds of the countryside and harvest. Both its incantatory and descriptive qualities work strongly on an audience, especially since immediate dramatic issues are in abeyance. To Jacobean audiences the hieroglyph, or intention, of the masque would have been clear. Iris presages the royal presence of Juno, queen of heaven and protector of marriages. She also represents the rainbow, token of the covenant whereby the Almighty, after showing his anger in the flood that had almost destroyed creation, had promised "seedtime and harvest" to mankind (*Genesis*, viii.22, ix.12-13). So, here, Iris represents Prospero's promise to bless the lovers after inflicting the tempest upon them. By calling "rich Ceres" (l. 75), Iris establishes at once that a full blessing is to be bestowed.

In Jacobean performances, a trapdoor in the ceiling above the stage (called "the heavens") would open at line 72, on mention of divine "grace". A machine would then begin to lower a chariot drawn by peacocks, in which stood Juno. At the same time, Ceres would begin her entry at stage level. With dancelike, stately movements appropriate to each personage, and accompanied by the soft music, the three goddesses prepare for the meeting which will be the first visual climax of the masque.

When Prospero refers later (l. 151) to the "fabric" of the masque, he certainly refers to Juno's chariot and the rich costumes, but he may also speak more precisely of some scenic devices. When *The Tempest* was performed at the Court of King James I, it may have utilized painted scenery provided from some earlier masque and representing a more than naturally exotic "Paradise" (see l. 124).

76-102 At line 76, Ceres speaks in recognition and

Her and her blind boy's scandaled° company   90
I have forsworn.

IRIS   Of her society
Be not afraid: I met her deity
Cutting° the clouds towards Paphos,° and her son
Dove-drawn° with her. Here thought they to have done
Some wanton charm upon this man and maid,   95
Whose vows are, that no bed-right shall be paid
Till Hymen's torch be lighted.° But in vain;
Mars's hot minion° is returned again;
Her waspish-headed son has broke his arrows,
Swears he will shoot no more, but play with sparrows,°   100
And be a boy right out.°

                        JUNO *alights.*

CERES   Highest queen of state,
Great Juno comes; I know her by her gait.

JUNO   How does my bounteous sister? Go with me
To bless this twain, that they may prosperous be
And honored in their issue.°   105
       (Sings.) Honor, riches, marriage-blessing,
                Long continuance, and increasing,
                Hourly joys be still° upon you!
                Juno sings her blessings on you.

CERES *(Sings)* Earth's increase,° foison° plenty,   110
                Barns and garners° never empty,
                Vines with clust'ring bunches growing,
                Plants with goodly burden bowing;
                Spring come to you at the farthest
                In the very end of harvest!°   115
                Scarcity and want shall shun you,
                Ceres' blessing so is on you.

FERDINAND   This is a most majestic vision, and
Harmonious charmingly.° May I be bold
To think these spirits?

PROSPERO   Spirits, which by mine art   120
I have from their confines° called to enact
My present fancies.°

disreputable

cutting through (in Cyprus, sacred to Venus)

(doves drew Venus's chariot)

until the marriage night

lustful mistress (Venus)

(associated with Venus, and symbols of lechery)

fully

fortune, offspring

continually

produce/progeny har-
vest/vigor

granaries

i.e., may you never experience winter

magically, fascinating*

prisons, proper territories

whims/fantasies/imaginative
thoughts

greeting. The purpose of her question (ll. 82-83) is to make the meaning of the masque explicit and to relate it—as was Jacobean custom—to the princely persons in whose honor it is being performed. A further question allows Iris to reflect the present moment by reminding Ferdinand of the "vows" he has just made. (This, of course, also enacts Prospero's "present fancies" in their idealism and fear.) These tasks completed, the appropriate moment for Juno to "alight" from her chariot has arrived (l. 102): the music changes and Iris and Ceres greet the queen with stately obeisance.

Ceres, who wishes all the "blessing" of the earth on the betrothed pair, has the crowning part in the masque (ll. 110-15), presenting her blessing after Juno herself has done so. At line 167, Ariel either says that he has performed this role himself, or else he refers to the whole masque by the name of *Ceres*, the former is the more likely sense of his words; both imply the central importance of Ceres and her blessing.

In calming the fears (see l. 92) of Ceres, the superior goddess, Iris describes Venus as "Mars's hot minion" and not as the goddess of "love" (as the lovers of *A Midsummer Night's Dream* had done); in this she will reflect Prospero's ideas about sexual desire, or the way in which he wishes to represent it to the young lovers. Lines 99-101, suggest that no one will ever again fall in love under the influence the "blind boy" Cupid (l. 90).

103-17 After greeting her sister, Ceres, Juno leads a procession of three toward the watching couple. The music changes again, and Juno and Ceres sing their appropriate blessings. They address Ferdinand and Miranda directly, offering their paradisal world to the young lovers. Assonance, internal rhymes and double-rhymed line-endings in these octosyllabics give a compact impression of authority and timelessness to these pronouncements. All the dramatic issues of the play itself are liable to be forgotten by the theater audience: these singers and dancers are "other" creatures, establishing their own reality, style and sense of time. This is both the heart of the masque and the most still moment of *The Tempest*.

So glowing is the impression of great sensuous riches and long-lasting honor, that the fanciful notion that winter shall be banished from the year's cycle of seasons may scarcely be noted by the audience, although Ferdinand's next words suggest that he is aware of the other-worldly nature of what he is being promised (see next note).

FERDINAND   Let me live here ever;
So rare a wond'red° father and a wise
Makes this place Paradise.

JUNO and CERES whisper, and send IRIS on employment.

PROSPERO   Sweet now, silence!
Juno and Ceres whisper seriously;   125
There's something else to do. Hush and be mute,
Or else our spell is marred.

IRIS   You nymphs, called Naiades,° of the windring° brooks,
With your sedged° crowns and ever-harmless° looks,
Leave your crisp° channels, and on this green land   130
Answer your summons; Juno does command.
Come temperate° nymphs, and help to celebrate
A contract of true love; be not too late.

Enter certain NYMPHS.

You sunburned sicklemen, of August weary,
Come hither from the furrow, and be merry.   135
Make holiday: your rye-straw hats put on,
And these fresh° nymphs encounter everyone
In country footing.°

Enter certain REAPERS, properly habited. They join with the NYMPHS in a graceful dance, towards the end whereof PROSPERO starts suddenly, and speaks; after which, to a strange, hollow, and confused noise, they heavily° vanish.

PROSPERO   *[Aside]* I had forgot that foul conspiracy
Of the beast Caliban and his confederates   140
Against my life. The minute of their plot
Is almost come. *[To the SPIRITS]* Well done! Avoid!° No more!

FERDINAND   This is strange. Your father's in some passion°
That works° him strongly.

MIRANDA   Never till this day
Saw I him touched with anger so distempered.°   145

PROSPERO   You do look, my son, in a moved sort,°

to be wondered at

118-24   During this duologue, the masquers probably dance in celebration. Ferdinand speaks as if in
the presence of some exceptional, paradisal experience, but turns instinctively to Prospero for explanation. Probably he is ill at ease, even fearful; see "May
I be bold...."
Miranda still has not spoken in this scene.
Possibly lines 123-24 are addressed to her so that
she is about to reply when her father intervenes with
"Sweet now, silence!"

water nymphs   winding*(?)
made of sedges   ever-inno-
cent
clear/rippling

chaste

eager, pure
dancing

clumsily, dejectedly (?)

125-42   Nymphs, representing chastity ("ever harmless" and "temperate," ll. 129, 132) as well as water
and air, and then sicklemen, representing fruitfulness
as well as fire and earth, are invoked in contrasting
verbal rhythms. They enter in contrasting processional dances, each provided with appropriate music,
and join together to dance a series of "encounters"
which develop into a celebration of concord and of
free union. They may follow the conventions of court
masques of this time by inviting Ferdinand and
Miranda to join their emblematic dance; but this is not
required by the stage directions of the first edition.
     As this celebration is about to reach its climax,
Prospero unexpectedly steps onto the stage-within-
the-stage and, suddenly, everything stops.
     While he speaks, Prospero probably holds his
staff aloft, causing everyone on stage to be frozen in
their various positions, "spell-stopped" (see V.i.61).
At the end of line 142, he orders the masquers away
and with a "confused noise" (echoing the sound of
the shipwreck, see I.i.54), they all "heavily vanish."
Prospero is left alone at center-stage, torn by his
passion (see l. 143), too angry for further words.
Miranda says, quite specifically, that he has never
looked like this before (see ll. 144-45). The play itself
seems to founder, like a ship driven on rocks at sea;
and it is clear that this destructive impulse has
sprung from Prospero's own mind.
     In the aftermath, Ferdinand and Miranda com-
ment apprehensively, but they cannot speak to
Prospero or offer any assistance. Both are deeply
affected and disturbed (see ll. 146-47).

go away

deep feeling
effects, moves

troubled, out of temper

agitated state of mind

146-63   Although passionately involved (see ll. 144-
45), Prospero speaks gently to Ferdinand, as if con-

As if you were dismayed. Be cheerful, sir,
Our revels° now are ended. These our actors,
As I foretold you, were all spirits, and
Are melted into air, into thin air;   150
And, like the baseless° fabric° of this vision,
The cloud-capped towers, the gorgeous palaces,
The solemn temples, the great globe itself,
Yea, all which it inherit,° shall dissolve,
And, like this insubstantial pageant faded,   155
Leave not a rack° behind. We are such stuff
As dreams are made on; and our little life
Is rounded° with a sleep. Sir, I am vexed.
Bear with my weakness; my old brain is troubled.
Be not disturbed with my infirmity.   160
If you be pleased, retire into my cell,
And there repose. A turn or two I'll walk
To still my beating mind.

FERDINAND, MIRANDA   We wish your peace.
                           Exit FERDINAND *with* MIRANDA.
PROSPERO   Come with a thought. I thank thee, Ariel. Come!

Enter ARIEL.

ARIEL   Thy thoughts I cleave to. What's thy pleasure?

PROSPERO   Spirit,   165
     We must prepare to meet with° Caliban.

ARIEL   Ay, my commander. When I presented° Ceres,
     I thought to have told thee of it; but I feared
     Lest I might anger thee.

PROSPERO   Say again, where didst thou leave these varlets?°   170

ARIEL   I told you, sir, they were red-hot with drinking;
     So full of valor that they smote the air
     For breathing in their faces, beat the ground
     For kissing of their feet; yet always bending°
     Towards their project. Then I beat my tabor;°   175
     At which like unbacked° colts they pricked their ears,
     Advanced° their eyelids, lifted up their noses
     As° they smelt music. So I charmed° their ears

entertainment

without foundation* build-
ing/contrivance

occupy it

mist, cloud (pun on *wrack*, a
spelling of wreck)

completed*

cerned chiefly for him. At first he talks simply about the end of their "revels," as if it were to be expected. But he is drawn into his explanation, so that he remembers all the glories of the world along with the "baseless" fiction of his own most hopeful "fancies." His speech has energy and commanding authority, but also a number of dying falls that become increasingly effective until he speaks of a "little life" and its completion in a sleep that sounds painless. It can be spoken in contrasting ways: Prospero may regret the loss of all that is "gorgeous" and "solemn", wishing he could dream for ever; or he can devalue these seductive notions because they are insubstantial vanities. The rhythms and versification are best suited to the former interpretation.

After the philosophizing, rhythms change again as Prospero concludes by apologizing for himself and his "weakness", and by caring for Ferdinand's peace of mind. Abrupt phrases suggest, however, that Prospero's thoughts are now elsewhere; he may start walking " a turn or two" (l. 162) already.

Before leaving the stage, the young couple speak together, very simply, wishing Prospero the "peace" which obviously he has not yet regained after the "strong" working of his passion. They do not respond to what he has just said, but rather retreat in the face of obvious signs of suffering and a "beating" mind (l. 163).

164-87 Ariel's entry almost anticipates Prospero's summons; "I thank thee" suggests that Prospero expects to be obeyed before he has finished speaking. Perhaps Ariel's music sounds before his entry.

encounter (as an enemy)

acted (or produced the
    masque of)

ruffians

At line 166, the use of "we" shows that Prospero feels especially at one with his spirit at this urgent time. But Ariel, already aware of what has happened, is carefully submissive, addressing "my commander" and acknowledging an earlier fear of his "anger." In the silence following the half-line of verse, Prospero catches Ariel's cooler grasp of the situation and his "beating mind" becomes less highly wrought. He asks briskly for information and Ariel is free to report in his earlier style, taking active delight in the antics of perplexed and frustrated humanity, as if they were frightened and stupid animals (see "colts...calflike," ll. 176, 179).

proceeding
side drum
unridden
raised
as if   cast a spell on

With "my bird" (l. 184), Prospero is ready to share the spirit's dispassionate sense of humor and issues detailed orders. There is no hesitation now; and Ariel's "I go, I go" suggests quick obedience (l. 187).

That calflike they my lowing° followed through
Toothed° briers, sharp furzes, pricking goss,° and thorns   180
Which ent'red their frail shins. At last I left them
I' th' filthy mantled° pool beyond your cell,
There dancing up to th' chins, that° the foul lake
O'erstunk° their feet.

PROSPERO   This was well done, my bird.°
Thy shape invisible retain thou still.   185
The trumpery° in my house, go bring it hither
For stale° to catch these thieves.

ARIEL   I go, I go.   *Exit.*

PROSPERO   A devil, a born devil, on whose nature
Nurture° can never stick; on whom my pains,
Humanely taken, all, all lost, quite lost.   190
And as with age his body uglier grows,
So his mind cankers. I will plague them all,
Even to roaring.

Enter ARIEL, *loaden with glistering apparel, etc.*

Come, hang them on this line.°

*[*PROSPERO *and* ARIEL *remain, invisible.] Enter* CALIBAN, STEPHANO, *and*
TRINCULO, *all wet.*

CALIBAN   Pray you tread softly, that the blind mole may not
Hear a footfall. We now are near his cell.   195

STEPHANO   Monster, your fairy, which you say is a harmless fairy,
has done little better than played the Jack° with us.

TRINCULO   Monster, I do smell all horse piss, at which my nose is
in great indignation.

STEPHANO   So is mine. Do you hear, monster? If I should take a 200
displeasure° against you, look you—

TRINCULO   Thou wert but a lost monster.

CALIBAN   Good my lord, give me thy favor still.
Be patient, for the prize I'll bring thee to

i.e., as a mother cow

jagged   gorse

covered with scum
so that
stunk more than*

darling

worthless finery,* trash
bait

education

clothesline/lime tree (?)

knave/will-o'-the-wisp

(pompous)

188-93 Once the spirit has gone, Prospero's passion again shows itself in castigating Caliban. But its energy is different now, expressed in intensifying repetitions, rather than images of insubstantial pageants. Sharply and bitterly, he acknowledges his own defeat and loss, and the hopelessness of his efforts to change a "born devil." He terminates this line of thought by resolving to punish all offenders—not only Caliban—until they roar like beasts (ll. 192-93). Having failed to reform or coerce Caliban before, he is ready for a further exercise of power. When Ariel returns with the "glistering appare," Prospero once again takes command and violence goes out of his speech.

It will take some time to hang the clothes on a line, so that the audience will have leisure to recall the other, more sophisticated test of the banquet which was set for the courtiers in III.iii: what reaction will be aroused by the display of finery and the outward manifestation of civilized and wealthy society?

The "line" on which the clothes are hung is either part of the setting for the scene, representing a tree, a part of the theater structure, or a stretched rope which Prospero causes to appear by magic (sometimes held up by attendant spirits). Ariel and Prospero stand to one side when their task is done, or on the upper level of the stage (see commentary at III.i.15-31).

194-213 The victims enter transformed by their time in the "filthy mantled pool" (l. 182), and with hangovers and ill tempers. Caliban, knowing that the time and place for murder have both come, is alert to danger, watchful and urgent; he speaks in a forceful whisper. Stephano and Trinculo, however, expostulate noisily. Stephano still retains something of his assumed regality, but at line 201 he halts in midsentence, as though he has lost all track of his thoughts; or perhaps he cannot find Caliban to chastise him, or he belches. Trinculo completes his sentence with melancholy brevity.

Caliban, who has answered none of the reproaches, now goes to Stephano to make another urgent plea, this time addressing him with reverence as his "lord" (l. 203). He continues in verse, against the current of the scene's prose. Stephano probably turns in anger towards him at the end of line 203, to be restrained only with difficulty and with promise of reward. Line 206 establishes a silence, that is perhaps fearful or poised for attack.

After the pause, indicated by the half verse-line, Trinculo begins another string of complaints, this

Shall hoodwink° this mischance. Therefore speak softly: 205
All's hushed as midnight yet.

TRINCULO   Ay, but to lose our bottles in the pool!

STEPHANO   There is not only disgrace and dishonor in that, monster, but an infinite loss.

TRINCULO   That's more to me than my wetting. Yet this is your 210
harmless fairy, monster.

STEPHANO   I will fetch off° my bottle, though I be o'er ears° for
my labor.

CALIBAN   Prithee, my king, be quiet. Seest thou here?
This is the mouth o' th' cell. No noise, and enter.   215
Do that good mischief which may make this island
Thine own forever, and I thy Caliban,
For aye thy footlicker.

STEPHANO   Give me thy hand. I do begin to have bloody thoughts.

TRINCULO   O King Stephano! O peer! O worthy Stephano, look 220
what a wardrobe here is for thee!

CALIBAN   Let it alone, thou fool! It is but trash.

TRINCULO   O, ho, monster! We know what belongs to a frippery.°
O King Stephano!

STEPHANO   Put off that gown Trinculo! By this hand, I'll have 225
that gown!

TRINCULO   Thy Grace shall have it.

CALIBAN   The dropsy drown this fool! What do you mean
To dote thus on such luggage?° Let't alone,
And do the murder first. If he awake,   230
From toe to crown he'll fill our skins with pinches,°
Make us strange stuff.

STEPHANO   Be you quiet, monster. Mistress line, is not this my
jerkin? *[Takes it down.]* Now is this jerkin under the line.°
Now, jerkin, you are like to lose your hair,° and prove a bald 235
jerkin.

hide from sight

retrieve   submerged

old-clothes shop

trash

bites/pleats

at the equator/under the lime
tree

(because of tropical fevers)

time about lack of drink. Stephano is distracted at
once, gathering heroic gestures and vaunts as he
fixes on the need for his bottle. Now he is ready for
action. He turns round to go out the way he entered.

214-19 Caliban has been growing still more impatient and apprehensive. Calling Stephano "my king"
for the first time, he at last gets attention. Perhaps
"Seest thou here?" makes Stephano think that his
bottle has been found; perhaps Caliban has dared to
shout—louder than anyone else—and that quietens
them all. As Stephano hesitates, Caliban presses his
advantage. Stephano is at last poised to act—might
his flight be barred by a quietly furious monster?—so
Caliban promises riches and abject homage; he may
kiss Stephano's foot (see l. 218).
  Now Stephano responds again to the vision of
power and takes Caliban's hand to mark his vow.
With "bloody thoughts," he swells in pride, oblivious
of his absurd, drunken and filthy, condition.

220-30 Searching for his bottle, Trinculo sees the
"glistering" clothes. He has not been interested in
Caliban's homage and is aware of no temptation (as
the courtiers *had* been when the banquet appeared
before them in III.iii): he accepts joyfully what is magically offered. Perhaps he gets a little frightened and
calls Stephano to join him, calling him "King" for the
first time. As he rushes to seize the nearest garment,
Caliban struggles to restrain him; but nevertheless
he starts to put on a cumbersome "gown" (l. 225).
  Stephano takes a moment to grasp the new situation, for his mind has been focused drunkenly on
mustering what "bloody thoughts" he could attain. By
line 225, however, he sees what Trinculo is doing
and crushingly orders him to stop. The fool is too
frightened to argue with the bully who is now at the
height of his royal success; he at once offers the
gown and begins a new struggle to take it off. In his
turn, Stephano begins to dress up, hampered by
being drunk and over-eager.
  Caliban is furious with Trinculo and in desperation and fear starts to argue with his king. He is
appalled at the pain he knows will be inflicted on
them all; his fear is such that he silences himself.
Only after the silence indicated by the half verse-line
(l. 232), does Stephano tell him to be quiet.

233-52 Having clambered into a gown, Stephano is
fully in command, ordering silence and condescend-
ing to make jokes to express his lordly and stupid
pleasure. He turns to get another garment off the
line.

TRINCULO   Do, do!° We steal by line and level,° and't like° Your
Grace.

STEPHANO   I thank thee for that jest. Here's a garment for't. Wit
shall not go unrewarded while I am king of this country. 240
"Steal by line and level" is an excellent pass of pate.° There's
another garment for't.

TRINCULO   Monster, come put some lime° upon your fingers, and
away with the rest.

CALIBAN   I will have none on't. We shall lose our time   245
And all be turned to barnacles,° or to apes
With foreheads villainous low.

STEPHANO   Monster, lay-to° your fingers; help to bear this away
where my hogshead of wine is, or I'll turn you out of my
kingdom. Go to, carry this.   250

TRINCULO   And this.

STEPHANO   Ay, and this.

A noise of hunters heard. Enter divers SPIRITS *in shape of dogs and hounds,
hunting them about;* PROSPERO *and* ARIEL *setting them on.*

PROSPERO   Hey, Mountain,° hey!

ARIEL   Silver!° There it goes, Silver!

PROSPERO   Fury, Fury! There, Tyrant, there! Hark, hark!   255
          *[*CALIBAN, STEPHANO, *and* TRINCULO *are driven out.]*
Go, charge my goblins that they grind their joints
With dry° convulsions, shorten up their sinews
With agèd° cramps, and more pinch-spotted make them
Than pard° or cat o' mountain.°

ARIEL   Hark, they roar!

PROSPERO   Let them be hunted soundly. At this hour   260
Lies at my mercy all mine enemies.
Shortly shall all my labors end, and thou
Shalt have the air at freedom. For a little,
Follow, and do me service.   *Exeunt.*

go on, go on   with measured
accuracy   if it please

sally (fencing term) of wit

birdlime (used for catching
birds; pun on *line*)

geese

set to work

Trinculo, who has probably hung back in fear of Stephano is rewarded ceremoniously with royal munificence. Stephano is so far gone in dreams of kingship, that he surveys his future rule and tops off one gift with another. Comic business climaxes as Stephano stumbles around in kingly trappings and heavy jocularity, and the fool is happily busy. Soon they can wear no more clothes and start piling more upon Caliban, using him as a beast of burden. They may have to chase him round the stage to achieve this, as Trinculo turns bully too.

The riotous disorder is counterstated by Caliban's fearful interjection and then by his silence. At a greater distance, Prospero and Ariel are watching quietly.

(name of hound)

quicksilver, mercury (poisonous)

severe

belonging to old age

leopard   panther

253-64   From offstage, the heavy breathing and yelping of hounds are heard. As the spirits in their new guise enter in a pack, Ariel and Prospero become huntsmen, "setting them on" by calling out their ominous names and possibly by using whips. The conspirators freeze with horror as the hounds bear down on them. For a time the stage is full of the sound and fury of dark savagery. Then the hounds, comics, glistering apparel and everything else is swept offstage, leaving Prospero giving precise orders to Ariel to ensure that the torment will continue and increase.

As Ariel delights in the roaring (see l. 259), Prospero is coolly aware of his "hour" and of his complete control over his "enemies." He is free to think of the end of his labors and of parting with Ariel. Master and servant leave together in a silence that carries promise of further manifestations of power.

ACT V

Scene i   *Enter* Prospero *in his magic robes, and* Ariel.

Prospero   Now does my project° gather to a head:°
My charms crack not, my spirits obey, and time
Goes upright with his carriage° How's the day?

Ariel   On the sixth hour, at which time, my lord,
You said our work should cease.

Prospero   I did say so,   5
When first I raised the tempest. Say, my spirit,
How fares the king, and's followers?

Ariel   Confined together
In the same fashion as you gave in charge,°
Just as you left them—all prisoners, sir,
In the line° grove which weather-fends° your cell.   10
They cannot budge till your release.° The king,
His brother, and yours, abide all three distracted,°
And the remainder mourning over them,
Brimful of sorrow and dismay; but chiefly
Him that you termed, sir, the good old Lord Gonzalo—   15
His tears runs down his beard like winter's drops
From eaves of reeds.° Your charm so strongly works° 'em,
That if you now beheld them, your affections°
Would become tender.

Prospero   Dost thou think so, spirit?

Ariel   Mine would, sir, were I human.

Prospero   And mine shall.   20
Hast thou, which art, but air, a touch,° a feeling
Of their afflictions, and shall not myself,
One of their kind, that relish° all as sharply
Passion° as they, be kindlier° moved than thou art?
Though with their high wrongs I am struck to th' quick,   25
Yet with my nobler reason 'gainst my fury
Do I take part. The rarer° action is
In virtue than in vengeance. They being penitent,
The sole drift° of my purpose doth extend

plan/alchemical process
ripen/come to its critical
phase
burden, load

commanded

lime   shelters*
freed by you
out of their senses

a thatched roof   affects
feelings

sympathy, response

feel*, partake of

powerful feeling   more gently (pun on *kind* = human
nature)

purer/less common

aim

1-7 Between Acts IV and V there is a pause, for
Prospero leaves the stage to return dressed in his
magic robes. Either the hunting continues off stage,
with yelps and roaring (possibly the hounds return
with their victims for a comic chase around the
stage), or solemn music is played to accompany the
offstage ceremonial robing.
  On re-entry, Prospero's passionate "anger" (see
IV.i.143-45) and his concern with torture (see
IV.i.256-60) have gone: now he is alert, confident
and almost inscrutable. He is neither anxious as he
asks about the time, nor recessive when Ariel
reminds him of promised freedom. He is fully in command.

7-32 Ariel answers with the sprightliness of his ear-
liest speeches, until he describes Gonzalo. Then
rhythm, imagery, and assonance are all highly sensitive and join to give a sustained impression of careful, sympathetic empathy. Then he probably looks at
his stern master in puzzlement or challenge (ll. 17-
19). Undoubtedly, Prospero's next question is
unprecedented: he is caught between wonder,
incredulity and a dawning self-realization. This is the
most intimate moment in the play, and the actors
must seek out the most appropriate way to play it
according to the growth of their characters and their
relationship to each other. It will be differently judged
every time the play is performed.
  Perhaps Prospero romanticizes in supposing
that Ariel has human feelings and is projecting his
own instinctive move toward forgiveness.
  Some Ariels almost cry here or look away; others taunt or accuse their masters; a few mark the
contrast between their responses by laughing on
their reply (l. 20). However the interchange is played,
the three words with which Prospero replies (l. 20)
mark a huge change. Perhaps he then walks away
and takes time before continuing; or he is heartened
and freed by his decision, and enjoys a rivalry in kindness with the spirit. At line 25, Prospero is resolved
to "become tender" (l. 19), though still aware of his
"fury" and hopes of "vengeance."
  By lines 31-32, Prospero can foresee the end of
the play and the fullness of his own renunciation of
power. Perhaps his last word, "themselves," implies
that he will no longer be the judge, admonisher and
instrument of punishment for other people, but only a

Not a frown further. Go release them, Ariel.   30
My charms I'll break, their senses I'll restore,
And they shall be themselves.

ARIEL   I'll fetch them, sir.   *Exit.*

PROSPERO   Ye elves of hills, brooks, standing° lakes and groves,
And ye that on the sands with printless foot
Do chase the ebbing Neptune, and do fly him   35
When he comes back; you demi-puppets° that
By moonshine do the green sour ringlets° make,
Whereof the ewe not bites; and you whose pastime
Is to make midnight° mushrooms, that rejoice°
To hear the solemn curfew: by whose aid—   40
Weak masters though ye be—I have bedimmed
The noontide sun, called forth the mutinous winds,
And 'twixt the green sea and the azured vault
Set roaring war; to the dread rattling thunder
Have I given fire, and rifted° Jove's stout oak°   45
With his own bolt;° the strong-based promontory
Have I made shake, and by the spurs° plucked up
The pine and cedar; graves at my command
Have waked their sleepers, oped, and let 'em forth
By my so potent art. But this rough° magic   50
I here abjure; and when I have required°
Some heavenly music—which even now I do—
To work mine end upon their senses that°
This airy charm is for, I'll break my staff,°
Bury it certain fathoms in the earth,   55
And deeper than did ever plummet sound
I'll drown my book.   *Solemn music.*

Here enters ARIEL *before; then* ALONSO, *with a frantic° gesture, attended by*
GONZALO; SEBASTIAN *and* ANTONIO *in like manner, attended by* ADRIAN *and*
FRANCISCO. *They all enter the circle which* PROSPERO *had made, and there*
stand charmed; which PROSPERO *observing, speaks.*

A solemn air, and the best comforter
To an unsettled fancy,° cure thy brains,
Now useless, boiled within thy skull. There stand,°   60
For you are spell-stopped.

few lines before he was insisting that enemies had to be "penitent" (l. 28) before his purpose could be satisfied. The action of the play hangs upon this requirement; and with this thought, Prospero dismisses Ariel and awaits developments.

still, not flowing

33-57 As Ariel leaves, Prospero turns to address the creatures he has commanded; to him they are real and always present. His invocations are delicate and responsive to natural phenomena, but then, with strengthening rhythms, he remembers the power these spirits have enabled him to wield: tempest, thunder, violence, and supernatural events. Prospero grows in force and presence during this speech, until he stands like "god of power" (see I.ii.10), who has caused graves to open and the dead to rise—feats that he has not demonstrated during the play. Some pause is necessary at line 50, or some shattering tremor, for here he acknowledges his magic to be "rough", and he abjures it.

doll-sized elves*
i.e., fairy rings

appearing overnight
(because then they are free
to work)

The speech continues with different rhythms, with a careful concern for fulfilling his tasks, and a stern resolve. Images of overwhelming earth and fathomless seas express the death-like nature of the deprivation he proposes for himself. Prospero is now serious, tender and, probably, suffering, as he looks ahead to mercy and forgiveness.

split   (a tree sacred to Jove)
thunderbolt
roots

But, for the present, he retains his power; his staff is not yet broken, his book not destroyed. As the speech ends, the audience hears solemn music which manifests his continuing mastery.

crude, inadequate/material,
  not spiritual
requested

the senses of those whom
relinquish office (as magician).

58-64 The frenzied and maddened courtiers contrast with the magician who is resolved in his mind, and with the "solemn" music. Led by Ariel, they stumble on stage, out of control, and are drawn miraculously into the "circle."

mad, wild

Prospero marks the circle on the ground as they enter, or possibly during his invocation of the spirits at lines 33-40 or line 52. He is in complete control, the courtiers standing now like puppets wherever they have been placed, waiting for their master to animate them.

mental disorder
remain

After a silence at the half verse-line 61, Prospero realizes that he is weeping; he has become "tender" as Ariel had foretold at the sight of Gonzalo's tears. But this one friend has been charmed to stillness like the others and cannot respond; perhaps Prospero weeps in part because he is himself isolated.

Holy Gonzalo, honorable man,
Mine eyes, ev'n sociable to the show of thine,
Fall fellowly drops.° The charm dissolves apace;
And as the morning steals upon the night,   65
Melting the darkness, so their rising senses
Begin to chase the ignorant fumes that mantle°
Their clearer° reason. O good Gonzalo,
My true preserver, and a loyal sir°
To him thou follow'st, I will pay thy graces   70
Home° both in word and deed. Most cruelly
Didst thou, Alonso, use me and my daughter;
Thy brother was a furtherer in the act.
Thou art pinched for't now, Sebastian. Flesh and blood,
You, brother mine, that entertained ambition,   75
Expelled remorse° and nature,° whom, with Sebastian—
Whose inward pinches therefore are most strong—
Would here have killed your king: I do forgive thee,
Unnatural though thou art. Their understanding
Begins to swell, and the approaching tide   80
Will shortly fill the reasonable shore°
That now lies foul and muddy. Not one of them
That yet looks on me or would know me.° Ariel,
Fetch me the hat and rapier in my cell.
I will discase° me, and myself present   85
As I was sometime Milan.° Quickly, spirit!
Thou shalt ere long be free.

ARIEL   *(Sings and helps to attire him.)*
          Where the bee sucks, there suck I:
          In a cowslip's bell I lie;
          There I couch when owls do cry.   90
          On the bat's back I do fly
          After summer merrily.
          Merrily, merrily shall I live now
          Under the blossom that hangs on the bough.

PROSPERO   Why, that's my dainty° Ariel! I shall miss thee, 95
          But yet thou shalt have freedom. So, so, so.
          To the king's ship, invisible as thou art:
          There shalt thou find the mariners asleep
          Under the hatches. The master and the boatswain

responsive to the sight of your
eyes, mine weep in sym-
pathy/from equal cause

cover up

purer/less clouded

gentleman

fully repay your kindness/
virtues

compassion   natural feelings

i.e., their power of reason

or would recognize me (if he
could see me)

disrobe/unmask

formerly Duke of Milan

fine, precious

64-87 Slowly the court party comes back to full life, and Prospero's words show that he watches with sympathy and understanding. He moves among them recognizing first his "loyal" friend and then his enemies. Facing his brother is the last test of his forgiveness; here syntax and rhythms are disturbed, but "I do forgive thee" marks the victory of mercy.

When the behavior of the charmed men is almost normal again, Prospero orders his own transformation. He commands Ariel to act quickly and promises freedom yet again (ll. 86-87), as if he were now impatient and longing to be done.

88-96 As Prospero becomes a duke, dressed in the same manner as his enemies who stand before him—though not ready for a royal wedding—Ariel sings about spring-time in a minute world where happiness is continuous and overflowing. So the parting of ways is made clear to the audience in a sustained emblem or posed double-portrait. Prospero acknowledges briefly his pleasure in the spirit's happiness (l. 95), but his duke's robes and rapier now weigh upon him. "I shall miss thee" follows immediately: he knows the spirit will have "freedom," whereas he is about to accept great constraints.

"So, so, so" (l. 96) is an invitation to the actor; he may chose to mark the last details of his robing or to take pleasure in Ariel, sharing his sense of happiness.

97-103 Ariel's fluent reply to Prospero's careful instruction suggests an eager scenting of his own release, but the half verse-line 101 shows that he pauses before speaking. There is another pause when he has gone, before Gonzalo attains the ability to speak. Both pauses help to give an impression of being on the brink of discovery and change, and of well-judged power (see "enforce" and "presently," ll. 100, 101).

104-25 Prospero has been onstage in control of the action almost continuously since III.iii, but the recognitions that now follow proceed slowly, step by step, following the pace and understanding of Gonzalo and Alonso; only with regard to Sebastian and Antonio does Prospero force the pace (see ll. 126-29).

Gonzalo's first reaction, as he falls on his knees in prayer (ll. 105-6), is to hope for escape. No one has yet seen Prospero, who has probably been standing outside the circle he had marked on the stage. He now speaks directly to Alonso, revealing his name and title. Before anyone can react, he also embraces the king.

Being awake, enforce them to this place,   100
And presently,° I prithee.

ARIEL   I drink the air before me, and return
Or ere your pulse twice beat.   *Exit.*

GONZALO   All torment, trouble, wonder, and amazement
Inhabits here. Some heavenly power guide us   105
Out of this fearful country.

PROSPERO   Behold, sir king,
The wrongèd Duke of Milan, Prospero.
For more assurance that a living prince
Does now speak to thee, I embrace thy body,
And to thee and thy company I bid   110
A hearty welcome.

ALONSO   Whe'er° thou be'st he or no,
Or some enchanted trifle° to abuse° me,
As late I have been, I not know. Thy pulse
Beats, as of flesh and blood; and, since I saw thee,
Th' affliction of my mind amends, with which,   115
I fear, a madness held me. This must crave—
And if this be at all—a most strange story.°
Thy dukedom I resign,° and do entreat
Thou pardon me my wrongs.° But how should Prospero
Be living, and be here?

PROSPERO   First, noble friend,   120
Let me embrace thine age, whose honor cannot
Be measured or confined.

GONZALO   Whether this be
Or be not, I'll not swear.

PROSPERO   You do yet taste
Some subtleties° o' th' isle, that will not let you
Believe things certain. Welcome, my friends all.   125
[Aside to SEBASTIAN *and* ANTONIO*]* But you, my brace of
    lords, were I so minded,
I here could pluck° his Highness' frown upon you,
And justify° you traitors. At this time
I will tell no tales.

immediately

whether

trick of magic   deceive

this—if it is actually happening— will be the most difficult to account for

I give up my rights to homage
and tribute

wrongdoings against you

tricks, deceptions/elaborate
confections (as at banquet)

draw down

prove

Still bewildered, Alonso finds his voice to attempt verification. (There is scope for comedy here in performance, but Prospero's watchful concern and involvement inhibit its development.) Then, while still insecure and fearing "madness" (l. 116), he resigns his right to homage and tribute from Milan and asks for "pardon"; there is no argument about "wrongs".

Line 119 is either forced and hurried, or should be spoken as two half-lines with a strong pause between them: either way Alonso crucial request for pardon has shifted his sense of reality. No longer does he worry "if this be at all" (l. 117), but asks how it should be so.

Now Prospero can turn to Gonzalo, who may still be kneeling and needs reassurance; he says nothing to Alonso to explain how these events are managed and does not even acknowledge, in words, his resignation of the dukedom. Although he embraces the old councillor, he leaves him still unsure how to respond and turns to the whole company, deliberately calling those "friends" who have only a short time before been enemies.

Throughout all this the court party remain where they have been placed, still "spell-stopped", and Prospero moves among them in command within the magic circle. He refers to his power ironically as "some subtleties o' th' isle", conscious that this "rough" magic must cease before all essential issues are thoroughly resolved.

126-37 Purposefully, Prospero moves to Sebastian and Antonio and, in an aside, warns them that he knows more than he has yet said. When only Sebastian replies, probably in a muttered protest (l. 129), Prospero singles out his own brother. His "No" at the end of line 129 might, however, be a passionate but brief rejoinder to Sebastian, before turning to the more important confrontation. But, on the other hand, if Sebastian has spoken aside, unheard by others, the "No" could be meditative, more a following through of his own thoughts than a rejoinder to Sebastian.

In condemning his brother, Prospero also forgives him, without knowing whether he is penitent (contrast ll. 28-30, above). Perhaps the sight of his intransigency shows him there is no other course to take. Antonio says nothing: he probably stands stone-still as Prospero confronts him. But it is just possible that he has fallen on his knees as Prospero speaks to him or as Sebastian acknowledges the power of what he has said. This is a crucial moment in the development of the drama and, amazingly, Shakespeare has left it ambiguous in the written text. Each production and each performance will make it

SEBASTIAN   *[Aside]* The devil speaks in him.

PROSPERO   No.
   For you, most wicked sir, whom to call brother   130
   Would even° infect my mouth, I do forgive
   Thy rankest° fault—all of them; and require
   My dukedom of thee, which perforce, I know,
   Thou must restore.

ALONSO   If thou beest Prospero,
   Give us particulars of thy preservation;   135
   How thou hast met us here, whom three hours since
   Were wrecked upon this shore; where I have lost—
   How sharp the point of this remembrance is!—
   My dear son Ferdinand.

PROSPERO   I am woe° for't, sir.

ALONSO   Irreparable is the loss, and Patience   140
   Says it is past her cure.

PROSPERO   I rather think
   You have not sought her help, of whose soft grace°
   For the like loss I have her sovereign° aid,
   And rest myself content.

ALONSO   You the like loss?

PROSPERO   As great to me as late;° and supportable   145
   To make the dear° loss, have I means much weaker
   Than you may call to comfort you,° for I
   Have lost my daughter.

ALONSO   A daughter?
   O heavens, that they were living both in Naples,
   The king and queen there! That they were, I wish   150
   Myself were mudded in that oozy bed
   Where my son lies. When did you lose your daughter?

PROSPERO   In this last tempest. I perceive these lords
   At this encounter do so much admire°
   That they devour their reason, and scarce think   155
   Their eyes do offices of truth,° their words
   Are natural breath.° But howsoev'r you have
   Been justled from your senses, know for certain

fully (emphatic)

foulest/most ambitious

weigh differently, but the main point is that Prospero does utter the words pronouncing "I do forgive thee." The other characters on stage are now free to look and react as they wish, so the moment is witnessed publicly and attention of the theater audience is drawn to Antonio and Prospero inescapably.

Watching the confrontation between the two brothers, Alonso can still hardly believe what he sees and takes the initiative to ask for explanations. The circle is probably broken up at this point, so that Antonio and Sebastian withdraw together, watchful but not speaking again except in response to new revelations. Their continued presence onstage and their facile comments when Caliban and his fellows arrive (see II. 263-66) serve to remind the audience of the imperfections and instability of the play's "happy ending."

sorry

137-53 Remembering Ferdinand, Alonso is stricken with grief. He may break down in tears at line 150, as his whole life is revalued in the light of the mere idea of reconciliation and hope which the thought of Miranda evokes.

gentle mercy

supremely powerful

As Prospero responds gently, it becomes increasingly clear how Shakespeare has used this prolonged recognition scene to reveal Prospero to the audience by revealing him to himself. He has waited twelve years for revenge and yet at the last moment he finds that he is "woe" for what he has inflicted on Alonso (l. 139). There is a private sense of humor in these words, playing as they do on Alonso's ignorance that Ferdinand is alive, and this is developed in Prospero's next response in which he acknowledges that he has had to learn from "Patience" and to "rest...content" in the forgiveness of

as recent as yours

grievous/heartfelt

(Alonso still has one child,
    Claribel)

his enemies (ll. 142-44). The gentle irony with which he applies "loss" to his own as well as Alonso's experience, prepares for the simple reply "In this last tempest" (l. 153). These words can sound grave and profound as Prospero remembers that the tempest was of his own making. But if the humor implicit in his preceding speeches has been played strongly enough, this last reply will be more resigned and self-critical: Prospero may be well aware of the other tempest within himself, using the words to express his sense of exhaustion and completion. This "tempest" is his struggle with anger and his renunciation of what he most had cherished—his art, his servant-spirit, and

wonder

his daughter. A further possibility is that "In this last tempest" is spoken with a laugh, and so played that it leads into (rather than contrasts with) Prospero's amusement at the "justled" senses of the lords (l. 158).

function truthfully

ordinary speech

That I am Prospero, and that very duke
Which was thrust forth of Milan, who most strangely   160
Upon this shore, where you were wrecked, was landed
To be the lord on't. No more yet of this;
For 'tis a chronicle of day by day,°
Not a relation for a breakfast, nor
Befitting this first meeting. Welcome, sir;   165
This cell's my court. Here have I few attendants,
And subjects none abroad. Pray you look in.
My dukedom since you have given me again,
I will requite you with as good a thing;
At least bring forth° a wonder° to content ye   170
As much as me my dukedom.

Here PROSPERO *discovers*° FERDINAND *and* MIRANDA *playing at chess.*

MIRANDA   Sweet lord, you play me false.

FERDINAND   No, my dearest love,
    I would not for the world.°

MIRANDA   Yes, for a score of kingdoms° you should wrangle,
    And I would call it fair play.

ALONSO   If this prove   175
    A vision of the island, one dear son
    Shall I twice lose.

SEBASTIAN   A most high miracle!

FERDINAND   Though the seas threaten, they are merciful.
    I have cursed them without cause.   *[Kneels.]*

ALONSO   Now all the blessings
    Of a glad father compass thee about!°   180
    Arise, and say how thou cam' st here.

MIRANDA   O wonder!
    How many goodly creatures are there here!
    How beauteous mankind is! O brave° new world
    That has such people in't!

PROSPERO   'Tis new to thee.

for telling on successive days

give birth to/present (on
    stage)   (pun on *Miranda*)

displays to view (theatrical
    term)

on any account

(wordplay on *world*, line 173)

surround you

fine

153-71 Without explaining his purpose, Prospero turns to the lords who have said nothing so far. Having reminded them of their helplessness, he proceeds to reaffirm the essential facts about himself and his preservation. The reference to "their words" (l. 156) may imply that the onlookers had begun speaking among themselves during the earlier part of this scene, their speeches being unscripted, without order, and given no attention by the principal characters. Now, at any rate, he allows no comment, but plays down the significance of what he has said with a buoyant, even jocular, conversational tone. Almost mischievously, with ironically polite modesty—remember that everyone present has been within his power—he refers to the cell-cave as his "court" and draws attention to the paucity of his courtiers and "subjects." He is in charge once more and, as if he were a dramatist deciding how a comedy should be concluded, he moves upstage toward the curtains which conceal an inner stage. Politely, he asks his audience to "look in" and then speaks once more as a magician (ll. 169-71). Perhaps he smiles as he announces the "wonder" he is about to reveal: two happy human beings. Everyone faces upstage now, and is quiet.

172-81 The lovers are intent on chess, the royal game of love and war. They do not realize they are being watched as they tease each other. Perhaps in silence, at the end of the incomplete verse-line 173, they kiss.

To one view, their "wrangling" is an intimation of renewed aggression and insecurity, an embryonic repetition of the initial conflicts of the play's action. The audience onstage, however, is oblivious of this, and the endearments that both use imply that the two chess-players are oblivious of it too. Even Sebastian seems caught up in a sense of wonder. All stand back until the lovers become aware of their presence. Ferdinand then runs to kneel before his father and is embraced.

181-84 Miranda's cry of wonder focuses attention back to her, as she awakens to a "brave new world." The irony of her taking the men assembled before her as "beauteous" is obvious to an audience and usually raises laughter as well as a troubled realization of her unpreparedness to join that older world.

Her lines are capable of many different readings. Sometimes she is happily awestruck: seeing a stage full with men, "How *many* goodly creatures..." can be accompanied with gleeful laughter. Or she may rise with calm confidence, giving her best attention to the dawn of a creation which she assumes to

ALONSO   What is this maid with whom thou wast at play?   185
   Your eld'st° acquaintance cannot be three hours.
   Is she the goddess that hath severed us,
   And brought us thus together?

FERDINAND   Sir, she is mortal;
   But by immortal° providence she's mine.
   I chose her when I could not ask my father   190
   For his advice, nor thought I had one. She
   Is daughter to this famous Duke of Milan,
   Of whom so often I have heard renown°
   But never saw before; of whom I have
   Received a second life; and second father   195
   This lady makes him to me.

ALONSO   I am hers.°
   But, O, how oddly will it sound that I
   Must ask my child forgiveness!

PROSPERO   There, sir, stop.
   Let us not burden our remembrances with
   A heaviness° that's gone.

GONZALO   I have inly wept,   200
   Or should have spoke ere this. Look down, you gods,
   And on this couple drop a blessèd crown!
   For it is you that have chalked forth° the way
   Which brought us hither.

ALONSO   I say amen, Gonzalo.

GONZALO   Was Milan° thrust from Milan that his issue   205
   Should become kings of Naples? O rejoice
   Beyond a common joy, and set it down
   With gold on lasting pillars: in one voyage
   Did Claribel her husband find at Tunis,
   And Ferdinand her brother found a wife,   210
   Where he himself was lost; Prospero his dukedom
   In a poor isle; and all of us ourselves,
   When no man was his own.°

ALONSO   *[To* FERDINAND *and* MIRANDA*]*   Give me your hands.
   Let grief and sorrow still embrace° his heart
   That doth not wish you joy.

longest

(wordplay on *mortal*, line 188)

report, praise

her father-in-law

sorrow/burden

marked out

Prospero

master of himself

always fasten around

be as well suited to her dreams as Ferdinand had proved to be. Or "wonder" may lend intensity to her words, so that she kneels solemnly before her father's treacherous brother, thinking him "beauteous." As Prospero acknowledges the ironies with "'Tis new to thee" he expresses his own troubled involvement, an instinct to protect his daughter, and a knowledge that he cannot do so. He may move to her side, or begin to do so and then hold back. Prospero's thoughts are no longer fully expressed in sustained speech at this point in the play: the audience is not shown all the workings of his mind, so that its attention is drawn more readily to the whole stage picture; so Prospero will be known, as he must know himself, in the relationship to the whole consort of characters.

185-98 For a moment Alonso is uncomprehending and alarmed; he forgets Prospero's talk of a daughter and his mastery of the situation. It is easiest for him to assume that Miranda is the "goddess" who raised the tempest, because this can account for his continued perplexity. As quickly as he can, Ferdinand reassures his father, confident that "providence" (not Prospero) and his own choice (not Ariel's prompting) had achieved his conquest. He brings Miranda to Alonso who then affirms the betrothal with the fewest possible words (l. 196). But he is possessed again by his sense of guilt: probably he weeps.

198-204 When Prospero intervenes, Gonzalo steps forward and breaks a long silence. He is so deeply moved that he speaks with difficulty at first. As he invokes the gods, he kneels or raises his arms to heaven.

Alonso's "amen" is spoken fervently; if it is also quiet, the king seems moved with a new humility. The courtiers probably echo his words.

205-15 Gonzalo grows in confidence as public spokesman. In performance, for all the importance of its dramatic position, this speech is uncertain in effect. Few actors can play Gonzalo in earlier scenes with sufficient assurance and self-knowledge to make this optimistic account of the play's action ring strong and true. As Alonso recognizes (and reminds the audience), Gonzalo forgets the still-evident signs of "grief and sorrow"; and he leaves both Antonio and Sebastian out of the reckoning. Gonzalo's insistence upon uncommon "joy" may even raise laughter because of his sanguine optimism. However if the actor establishes Gonzalo's respect for the "gods" (l. 201) and shows him struggling to restrain tears as he

GONZALO   Be it so! Amen.   215

Enter ARIEL, *with the* MASTER *and* BOATSWAIN *amazedly following*

O look sir, look sir, here is more of us!
I prophesied, if a gallows were on land,
This fellow could not drown. Now blasphemy,
That swear'st grace o'erboard,° not an oath on shore?
Hast thou no mouth by land? What is the news?   220

BOATSWAIN   The best news is that we have safely found
Our king and company; the next, our ship,
Which, but three glasses since,° we gave out split,
Is tight and yare° and bravely rigged, as when
We first put out to sea.

ARIEL   [*Aside to* PROSPERO] Sir, all this service   225
Have I done since I went.

PROSPERO   [*Aside to* ARIEL]   My tricksy° spirit!

ALONSO   These are not natural events; they strengthen°
From strange to stranger. Say, how came you hither?

BOATSWAIN   If I did think, sir, I were well awake,
I'd strive to tell you. We were dead of sleep   230
And—how we know not—all clapped° under hatches;
Where, but even now, with strange and several° noises
Of roaring, shrieking, howling, jingling chains,
And moe° diversity of sounds, all horrible,
We were awaked; straightway at liberty;   235
Where we, in all our trim,° fleshly beheld
Our royal, good, and gallant ship, our master
Cap'ring to eye° her. On a trice,° so please you,
Even in a dream, were we divided from them°
And were brought moping° hither.

ARIEL   [*Aside to* PROSPERO]   Was't well done?   240

PROSPERO   [*Aside to* ARIEL] Bravely, my diligence.° Thou shalt be
free.

ALONSO   This is as strange a maze as e'er men trod,
And there is in this business more than nature

speaks of "joy" (l. 207), he may win the right to sum up everyone's experience. Gonzalo's last summing-up (ll. 212-13) echoes New Testament teaching (e.g., *John*, xii.25) and also Prospero's hard-won enlightenment (see l. 153 and commentary on ll. 137-53). Alonso follows immediately with thoughts of the young couple to whom he offers a formal benediction; this is affirmed around the stage, Gonzalo taking the lead. But these congratulations are halted by new arrivals.

who swore so much while at sea that all propriety was lost

215-40 Ariel leads in the master and the bosun who are still bemused from their odd adventures, and so a new comic impetus is given to the play's action. On top of their strange behavior, there is comedy in the way in which Gonzalo is so quick to take pride in his own percipience—possibly he laughs at this himself.

three hours ago

sound and ready for sea

But the bosun's tale serves to remind the audience of Prospero's unabated control over men's imaginations, which for the court party he has already forgone.

Alonso probably addresses his question to the master, who is responsible for the ship and its company. Either this officer is not sufficiently "awake" to answer, or the bosun is so high in spirits that he takes over from his superior, irrepressibly. In the latter case, the master may well join in with signs of agreement—or disagreement—during the next ten lines, especially at 237-38.

playful, clever

grow

240-41 These asides (and those at ll. 225-26) show that Ariel has left the mariners surrounded by the courtiers and now stands close to Prospero. Both wait to take the next steps in unraveling the plot. Prospero's new calm is accentuated by Ariel's requests for approval which are signs of his impatience as he waits for freedom (see l. 241). Prospero's first response (l. 226) shows that he shares his spirit's pleasure in tricking the good sense of zealous mortals; it is a pleasurable relief from his deeper involvement. But his second aside shows that he is once more aware of his responsibilities and the need to relinquish his power; he may envy, momentarily, Ariel's simpler capacity for happiness (see ll. 93-94), all "diligence" finished.

imprisoned

various

more

all prepared for sea

dancing to see   moment

the rest of the crew

in a daze

242-55 Alonso is once again lost in amazement. Prospero leaves Ariel to reassure him and to prepare for the next revelation. Towards the end of the masque, he had stepped in to stop proceedings as he remembered Caliban (see IV.i.139-41); now he steps back into the play's action and gently instructs his spirit to free the conspirators. (Everyone else may be "spell-stopped" meanwhile, to be aroused by

quick, industrious servant*

Was ever conduct of.° Some oracle
Must rectify our knowledge.

PROSPERO   Sir, my liege,   245
Do not infest° your mind with beating on
The strangeness of this business. At picked° leisure,
Which shall be shortly, single° I'll resolve° you,
Which to you shall seem probable, of every
These happened accidents. Till when, be cheerful   250
And think of each thing well. *[Aside to* ARIEL*]* Come hither,
    spirit.
Set Caliban and his companions free.
Untie the spell. *[Exit* ARIEL*.]* How fares my gracious sir?
There are yet missing of your company
Some few odd° lads that you remember not.   255

Enter ARIEL, *driving in* CALIBAN, STEPHANO, *and* TRINCULO, *in their stolen
apparel.*

STEPHANO   Every man shift for all the rest, and let no man take
    care for himself; for all is but fortune. *Coragio,*° bully-mon-
    ster,° *coragio!*

TRINCULO   If these be true spies° which I wear in my head, here's
    a goodly sight.   260

CALIBAN   O Setebos,° these be brave° spirits indeed!
How fine my master is! I am afraid
He will chastise me.

SEBASTIAN   Ha, ha!
What things are these, my Lord Antonio?
Will money buy 'em?

ANTONIO   Very like. One of them   265
Is a plain fish, and no doubt marketable.

PROSPERO   Mark but the badges° of these men, my lords,
Then say if they be true.° This misshapen knave,
His mother was a witch; and one so strong
That could control the moon, make flows and ebbs,   270
And deal in her command without her power.°
These three have robbed me, and this demi-devil—

responsible for

harass

chosen

alone/sincerely   inform, satisfy

extra/strange

courage (It.)

my fine monster

accurate observers

(the god worshipped by
    Caliban's mother)   splendid

signs of service

truly your servants/honest

make use of the moon's influence while not possessing a power equal to the moon's

---

Prospero when his instructions have been received.) Ariel, sensing his own impending freedom, leaves without a word.

256-58 Ariel had led in the mariners, but now he drives in the noisy, absurd, filthy and drunken trio who are almost unrecognizable beneath their dirt and the damaged finery they still wear or trail behind them (see ll. 298-99).

In the comic uproar, Stephano's outburst oddly echoes Gonzalo's concluding judgement (ll. 212-13). He has reversed the proverbial admonition "every man for himsel," so that he, too, recommends saving one's life by losing it. He stands as leader of the trio, blear-eyed, bruised, belligerent, and at a complete loss. He probably sees nothing of the company assembled around him but goes stomping around in pursuit of he knows not what.

259-63 Trinculo responds cautiously to what he sees dimly. He focuses as best he can, but is too timorous and too worn out to believe his good fortune. Caliban is the last to speak (his eyes may be covered by the many garments he has been forced to carry), but there is no ambiguity in what he says. For the first time in the play, he cries out to his mother's god, Setebos; so his earlier silence in this scene may be occupied with still more inarticulate, less civilized, responses. At first his sense of wonder is strongest (oddly it is not unlike Miranda's; see ll. 181-84), then of servitude, and then of fear.

263-66 No one has yet recognized the butler and fool; they must take over the stage so completely that no one has anything to say until Sebastian's acquisitive instinct surfaces out of his laughter. Possibly no one else has laughed and he is the first to break out of silent astonishment.

Antonio's reply provides his only words in Act V. The actor will be drawn to make as much as possible of it, showing either callow indifference, with a snub to Sebastian, or keen calculation of heartless exploitation. But it might be best to avoid any overstatement, preferring, rather, to maintain a very private course throughout the whole Act; so Antonio, although prompted to speak, still chooses to reveal as little as possible of his inner thoughts. But, of course, even such a refusal to participate will express his self: stubbornness, independence, distrust of his accomplice as well as his enemies.

267-76 Once more Prospero takes over. He focuses attention on Caliban and identifies him by his mother, witchcraft, bastardy and conspiracy. The

For he's a bastard one—had plotted with them
To take my life. Two of these fellows you
Must know and own; this thing of darkness I   275
Acknowledge mine.

CALIBAN   I shall be pinched to death.

ALONSO   Is not this Stephano, my drunken butler?

SEBASTIAN   He is drunk now. Where had he wine?

ALONSO   And Trinculo is reeling ripe. Where should they
Find this grand liquor that hath gilded 'em?   280
How cam'st thou in this pickle?°

TRINCULO   I have been in such a pickle,° since I saw you last, that
I fear me will never out of my bones. I shall not fear fly-
blowing.°

SEBASTIAN   Why, how now, Stephano?   285

STEPHANO   O, touch me not! I am not Stephano, but a cramp.°

PROSPERO   You'd be king o' the isle, sirrah?

STEPHANO   I should have been a sore° one then.

ALONSO   This is a strange thing as e'er I looked on.

PROSPERO   He is as disproportioned in his manners   290
As in his shape.—Go, sirrah, to my cell;
Take with you your companions. As you look
To have my pardon, trim it handsomely.

CALIBAN   Ay, that I will; and I'll be wise hereafter,
And seek for grace.° What a thrice-double ass   295
Was I to take this drunkard for a god
And worship this dull fool!

PROSPERO   Go to! Away!

ALONSO   Hence, and bestow your luggage where you found it.

SEBASTIAN   Or stole it rather.
                    [*Exeunt* CALIBAN, STEPHANO, *and* TRINCULO.]
PROSPERO   Sir, I invite Your Highness and your train   300
To my poor cell, where you shall take your rest
For this one night; which, part of it, I'll waste°

"misshapen knave" may lie as if dead, crouch further off, weep, cry out in frustration and anticipated pain; or he may seek to kiss Prospero's foot. When next he speaks (l. 276), he is possessed with fear.

As Prospero acknowledges Caliban as his responsibility, his voice will express his memory of "pains, humanely taken" that were quite lost (IV.i.189-90) and of the disruption of his radiant masque. "This thing of darkness", with its echo of the biblical "prince of darkness", seems to link Caliban in Prospero's thoughts with ultimate evil and destruction; by acknowledging him as his own, he may be confessing an inability to eradicate evil in himself, as in others.

mess

preservative (i.e., the foul pond water or the liquor)

i.e., he is so thoroughly pickled that flies will not lay eggs on him

a mass of violent pain

aching/tyrannical

pardon

spend

277-81 As Alonso begins to recall ordinary existence, Sebastian, who was about to take his life and seize his throne, is quick to be on the side of propriety and to be matter-of-fact about it. He has moved away from Antonio, to be close to his brother and talk with him, as if nothing unusual had occurred.

282-88 Trinculo and Stephano try to work their way back to favor with "sore" jokes at their own expense. Caliban watches them fixedly, with a dawning understanding of what he has done that only adds to the strangeness of his own behavior (see l. 289).

289-97 Alonso directs attention to the silent and probably trembling Caliban. Prospero gives curt orders and Caliban at once responds. As he stands again, almost human, he vows to seek that "grace" that Prospero had said could never be his (see IV.i.188-92). But then he stops, and for the first time mocks himself: he is perhaps tense with self-reproach, or loud in exasperation; or he might display a new aggression against his misleaders. Prospero does not react noticeably to this; he seems unyielding, ordering Caliban away, as if fit only for servitude.

Much depends on how Caliban reacts finally to Prospero, and how he leaves the stage. His wordless and lengthy exit can show the dawn of a new life, a zealous bullying of his two inferiors, a sense of defeat or incomprehension, or a dull acceptance of slavery and his fellow fools.

298-99 Sebastian is now established at Alonso's side and is quick to sharpen the moral edge of Alonso's reproof. Both these speeches counteract, and therefore accentuate, the comic aspects of the bedraggled and disorderly *exeunt*.

300-18 For the last time, Prospero takes the lead, speaking now of the future as well as the past. His

With such discourse as, I not doubt, shall make it
Go quick away—the story of my life,
And the particular accidents° gone by   305
Since I came to this isle. And in the morn
I'll bring you to your ship, and so to Naples,
Where I have hope to see the nuptial
Of these our dear-beloved solemnized;
And thence retire me to my Milan, where   310
Every third thought shall be my grave.°

ALONSO   I long
To hear the story of your life, which must
Take the ear strangely.°

PROSPERO   I'll deliver° all;
And promise you calm seas, auspicious gales,°
And sail so expeditious that shall catch°   315
Your royal fleet far off. *[Aside to ARIEL]* My Ariel, chick,
That is thy charge. Then to the elements
Be free, and fare thou well. *[To the others]* Please you, draw
near.   *Exeunt omnes.*

events

i.e., I will prepare myself for
  death

make strange hearing

tell

breezes

catch up with

manner is calm; his words are reserved, although
alive with small ironies directed at his own preten-
sions.

Most Prosperos give the last order and farewell
to Ariel with tender regret or even reluctance. They
can, however, be spoken freely, as if he now accepts
the loss.

The other characters may well be spell-stopped
for this encounter, giving Ariel scope to respond. But
he says nothing, and flies off, straight away, liberat-
ed as he had longed to be throughout the play. Some
Ariels laugh as they go, or sing; few do so much as
look at their master.

Allowing himself no pause, Prospero turns and
begs all present to "draw near" and so affirms his fel-
lowship with them. It will take some time for the
dramatis personae to file off the stage through the
entrance to Prospero's cell, so passing their host in
turn. Among the procession—perhaps the last member—is Antonio, but still Shakespeare has kept him
without words. The brothers sometimes refuse eye-
contact with each other, or Prospero attempts contact unsuccessfully. In other productions, they do
confront each other openly, so that Prospero has to
choose once more the "rarer action" without receiv-
ing sign of penitence (see ll. 25-30).

EPILOGUE

Spoken by PROSPERO

Now my charms are all o'erthrown,
And what strength I have's mine own,
Which is most faint. Now, 'tis true,
I must be here confined by you,
Or sent to Naples. Let me not,   5
Since I have my dukedom got
And pardoned the deceiver, dwell
In this bare island by your spell;
But release me from my bands°
With the help of your good hands.°   10
Gentle breath° of yours my sails
Must fill, or else my project fails,
Which was to please. Now I want°
Spirits to enforce, art to enchant;
And my ending is despair   15
Unless I be relieved by prayer,
Which pierces so that it assaults
Mercy itself, and frees all faults.
  As you from crimes would pardoned be,
  Let your indulgence set me free.   20

                                              Exit.

FINIS

1-20 Prospero turns from his cell and his guests, and walks towards the audience. He speaks both in character and as the actor stripped of his part and about to shed his costume. Both have lost their magic and now simple words and octosyllabic rhymed speech express a new dependence on the audience's acceptance. The re-emergence of the single figure as the others leave the stage gains closest attention, so that this epilogue can be spoken quietly and with deliberation.

In responding with applause, the audience identifies with Prospero's resignation of his art and with the player's attempt to embody one of the most deeply considered and sensitively felt of all of Shakespeare's characters. Like Ariel and Caliban, Prospero and the actor ask for freedom—freedom to be a man with only his own strength and with indulgence for his faults.

bonds/obligations

i.e., your clapping (to break the spell)

i.e., approving comment

lack

The reference to "prayer," the choice of the active verb "pierce," the reflection in "Mercy" and "free" of so many crises in the play itself, together with an allusion to the Lord's prayer in the last couplet, all widen the scope of the Epilogue and prepare for the direct challenge to "you," the audience. After a good performance, applause is an act of identification, an affirmation of hope against the most carefully wrought "despair." Before acknowledging the art of actor and character, each member of the audience is asked to be aware of roles in life outside the theater.

In performance, however, some actors stay entirely in character and use the Epilogue as another scene in the play. Then Prospero is still in the throes of "despair" (l. 15) and he is dependent on forgiveness for his autocratic employment of "rough magic" (V.i.50), until freed by applause. Sometimes he actually breaks his "staff" and drowns his "book" at the end of the speech. This single-minded interpretation has the disadvantage of endowing the audience with the authority of heavenly "Mercy;" it also loses the many ironies which are active throughout the Epilogue.

Another interpretation makes the Epilogue Shakespeare's own farewell to his art, as he began to think of retiring from the theater in London to live in rural Stratford-upon-Avon. On some occasions, the bookish duke of the last Act has been given the appearance of the Bard of Stratford, as known in his monument or the frontispiece of the first Folio edition of the plays.

However it is performed, this last appearance is a final effort after a long part, when the mask begins, at least, to drop. This man looks around afraid of being "confined" and knows his strength is now "most faint;" he looks in the eyes of the audience as he asks for "indulgence." The performance as a whole will dictate whether or not he smiles.

Textual Notes

The Tempest was not printed prior to 1623 when it was published in the Folio edition of Shakespeare's *Comedies, Histories, & Tragedies*. Here it was given pride of place, and the printer was given a specially prepared manuscript, probably written out and edited by Ralph Crane who often transcribed plays for the King's Men, the actors' company of which Shakespeare had been a member. There are very few verbal obscurities in this text, and the stage directions are fuller and more complete than is usual even in good Shakespeare texts. Quite exceptionally, both a description of the setting and a list of characters are provided at the end of the play, a feature common in the printing of Court masques but not of plays. The punctuation is unusually clear, but with an overuse of colons, semicolons, and commas; a comparison with texts set from autograph manuscripts suggests that Shakespeare's usually light and sensitive punctuation has been lost in the processes of preparing the printer's copy and of typesetting. (One of the most difficult tasks of an editor preparing a modernized text of this play for reading or performance is to lighten the pedantic heaviness of the Folio punctuation.)

The following collation lists all substantive departures from the Folio. The reading of the present edition is given first in italics, followed by the Folio reading in roman type.

I.ii.203 *lightnings* Lightning   284 *she* he   382 *the burden bear* beare the burthen

II.i.35 *ANTONIO* Seb.   36 *SEBASTIAN* Ant.

III.i.2 *sets* set   15 *least* lest

III.iii.2 *ache* akes   29 *islanders* Islands

IV.i.9 *off* of   13 *gift* guest   74 *her* here   110 *CERES* [F omits]   124, S.D. [after line 127]   193 *them on* on them   229 *Let't* let's

V.i.60 *boiled* boile   72 *Didst* Did   75 *entertained* entertaine   82 *lies* ly

SHAKESCENES: SHAKESPEARE FOR TWO

The Shakespeare Scenebook

EDITED AND WITH AN INTRODUCTION
BY JOHN RUSSELL BROWN

Thirty-five scenes are presented in newly edited texts, with notes which clarify meanings, topical references, puns, ambiguities, etc. Each scene has been chosen for its independent life requiring only the simplest of stage properties and the barest of spaces. A brief description of characters and situation prefaces each scene and is followed by a commentary which discusses its major acting challenges and opportunities.

paper ∎ ISBN 1-55783-049-5

APPLAUSE

SHAKESPEARE'S PLAYS IN PERFORMANCE
by John Russell Brown

In this volume, John Russell Brown snatches Shakespeare from the clutches of dusty academics and thrusts him centerstage where he belongs—in performance.

Brown's thorough analysis of the theatrical experience of Shakespeare forcibly demonstrates how the text is brought to life: awakened, colored, emphasized, and extended by actors and audiences, designers and directors.

"A knowledge of what precisely can and should happen when a play is performed is, for me, the essential first step towards an understanding of Shakespeare."
—*from the Introduction by John Russell Brown*

paper•ISBN 1-55783-136-X•$14.95

APPLAUSE

RECYCLING SHAKESPEARE

by Charles Marowitz

Marowitz' irreverent approach to the bard is destined to outrage Shakespearean scholars across the globe. Marowitz rejects the notion that a "classic" is a sacrosanct entity fixed in time and bounded by its text. A living classic, according to Marowitz, should provoke lively response—even indignation!

In the same way that Shakespeare himself continued to meditate and transform his own ideas and the shape they took, Marowitz gives us license to continue that meditation in productions extrapolated from Shakespeare's work. Shakespeare becomes the greatest of all catalysts who stimulates a constant reformulation of the fundamental questions of philosophy, history and meaning. Marowitz introduces us to Shakespeare as an active contemporary collaborator who strives with us to yield a vibrant contemporary theatre.

paper • ISBN: 1-55783-094-0

APPLAUSE

LIFE IS A DREAM
and Other SPANISH Classics
Edited by Eric Bentley
Translated by Roy Campbell

LIFE IS A DREAM
by Calderon de la Barca

FUENTE OVEJUNA
by Lope de Vega

THE TRICKSTER OF SEVILLE
by Tirso de Molina

THE SIEGE OF NUMANTIA
by Miguel de Cervantes

paper • ISBN: 1-55783-006-1

APPLAUSE

SOLILOQUY!
The Shakespeare Monologues
Edited by Michael Earley and Philippa Keil

At last, over 175 of Shakespeare's finest and most performable monologues taken from all 37 plays are here in two easy-to-use volumes (MEN and WOMEN). Selections travel the entire spectrum of the great dramatist's vision, from comedies and romances to tragedies, pathos and histories.

"Soliloquy is an excellent and comprehensive collection of Shakespeare's speeches. Not only are the monologues wide-ranging and varied, but they are superbly annotated. Each volume is prefaced by an informative and reassuring introduction, which explains the signals and signposts by which Shakespeare helps an actor on his journey through the text. It includes a very good explanation of blank verse, with excellent examples of irregularities which are specifically related to character and acting intentions. These two books are a must for any actor in search of a 'classical' audition piece."

ELIZABETH SMITH
Head of Voice & Speech
The Juilliard School

paper—MEN: ISBN 0-936839-78-3
WOMEN: ISBN 0936839-79-1

APPLAUSE

MEDIEVAL AND TUDOR DRAMA

Twenty-four Plays
Edited and with introductions
by John Gassner

The rich tapestry of medieval belief, morality and manners shines through this comprehensive anthology of the twenty-four major plays that bridge the dramatic worlds of medieval and Tudor England. Here are the plays that paved the way to the Renaissance and Shakespeare. In John Gassner's extensively annotated collection, the plays regain their timeless appeal and display their truly international character and influence.

Medieval and Tudor Drama remains the indispensable chronicle of a dramatic heritage — the classical plays of Hrotsvitha, folk and ritual drama, the passion play, the great morality play *Everyman*, the Interlude, Tudor comedies *Ralph Roister Doister* and *Gammer Gurton's Needle*, and the most famous of Tudor tragedies *Gorboduc*. The texts have been modernized for today's readers and those composed in Latin have been translated into English.

paper • ISBN: 0-936839-84-8

APPLAUSE

COMMEDIA IN PERFORMANCE SERIES

THE THREE CUCKOLDS
by Leon Katz
paper • ISBN: 0-936839-06-6

THE SON OF ARLECCHINO
by Leon Katz
paper • ISBN: 0-936839-07-4

CELESTINA
by Fernando do Rojas

Adapted by Eric Bentley

Translated by James Mabbe

paper • ISBN: 0-936839-01-5

APPLAUSE

THE ACTOR'S MOLIÈRE

A New Series of Translations for the Stage by

Albert Bermel

THE MISER and GEORGE DANDIN
ISBN: 0-936839-75-9

✳

THE DOCTOR IN SPITE OF HIMSELF
and THE BOURGEOIS GENTLEMAN

ISBN: 0-936839-77-5

✳

SCAPIN and DON JUAN
ISBN: 0-936839-80-5

APPLAUSE

THE ACTOR AND
THE TEXT
by Cicely Berry

As voice director of the Royal Shakespeare
Company, Cicely Berry has worked with actors such
as Jeremy Irons, Derek Jacobi, Jonathan Pryce, Sinead
Cusack and Antony Sher. *The Actor and The Text*
brings Ms. Berry's methods of applying vocal production skills within a text to the general public.

While this book focuses primarily on speaking
Shakespeare, Ms. Berry also includes the speaking of
some modern playwrights, such as Edward Bond.

As Ms. Berry describes her own volume in the
introduction:

" ... this book is not simply about making the
voice sound more interesting. It is about getting
inside the words we use ...It is about making the language organic, so that the words act as a spur to the
sound ..."

paper•ISBN 1-155783-138-6

APPLAUSE

THE APPLAUSE FIRST FOLIO OF SHAKESPEARE

Prepared & Annotated by Neil Freeman

"NEIL FREEMAN IS HANDING YOU THE SAME TEXT THAT WILLIAM SHAKESPEARE HANDED HIS ACTORS...DESTINED TO BECOME A STANDARD TEXT IN SCHOOLS, UNIVERSITIES AND LIBRARIES." —Tina Packer, Artistic Director *Shakespeare & Company*

The publication of the complete FIRST FOLIO OF SHAKESPEARE with all 36 plays in modern type (and at a non-scholarly, affordable price) allows readers for the first time to ponder and marvel at Shakespeare in the raw — with a little authoritative help from Neil Freeman, who painstakingly prepared and annotated the text.

Specially designed with a stay-flat, full-color leatherette binding.

ISBN 1-155783-333-8

APPLAUSE